BREAKING THE CODE

Winning Strategies for Women in Cybersecurity & Tech

DR. CHERYL COOPER

Author Website: https://www.drcherylcooper.com

Book Artwork: Bam SupremeReign (Tate Design Group)

Foreword: Edwige Robinson
Book Editor: Stephanie S. Johnson

Book Disclaimer: Names have been changed to protect the identity of individuals in the author's life story.

U.S. $24.99

DEDICATION

To Every Woman Who Has Ever Felt Invisible,

This book is for you. To my daughter, my granddaughter, and all the girls I have met—and those I have yet to meet—in a world that has systematically overlooked you because of your gender, ethnicity, or skin color, I see you. Your strength, resilience, and brilliance are the driving forces behind this work.

To all the girls and women searching for guidance, direction, a coach, or a mentor to help them navigate this wild world as a woman, this book is dedicated to you. May you find the courage to pursue your dreams and the wisdom to know your worth. It's time to step into your power!

ACKNOWLEDGEMENTS

Writing this book has taken me on a journey of discovery, self-inspiration, and growth. I want to express my deepest gratitude to Elizabeth Leiba, 2X best-selling author, and Sheila Kennedy, author and publisher, for believing in and guiding me through this process. Your mentorship and advice have been invaluable. From believing in the idea of the book at its inception to sharing your personal and professional insights on why the world needed to hear my story, I am forever thankful. Your unwavering support and friendship are priceless.

To my daughter, Kamilah, who is my rock and inspiration. Our love bond has emerged stronger through good times and bad. Your willingness to listen to my stories, provide candid feedback, and be my trusted ear is a treasure and blessing. I am so thankful to you and my grandchildren, who bring abundant joy and purpose to my life.

To Abraham, who stands by me through thick and thin. Your support and love are my anchor. You have been there for my wins and challenges, always offering a shoulder to lean on. Thank you for your continued faith in me.

Thank you to my parents, who are resting in heaven, my siblings, and family members who often remind me about the power and importance of sharing the good and the bad times in my life. Your relationships and stories have helped to shape my experiences and taught me extraordinary life lessons.

I am also indebted to the many women and high school girls I've mentored, my friends, male allies, and work colleagues for their unwavering support.

Special thanks to Glenda Garner, Adrienne Watson-Kent, Dr. Marge Sendze, Cynthia Newsome, Aaron Fulk, Joyce White, Naeem Babri, Christine Gordon, and Krina Snider, who accepted me for who I am and encouraged me throughout the writing process. Your positive affirmations and encouragement have been instrumental in helping me complete this book.

I am deeply humbled and honored that each of you has promoted me to others and provided a stage for me to shine.

This acknowledgment would also not be complete without recognizing the executive teams at the Fortune 100 and 500 companies I've served. Although this book underscores my struggles with diversity, inclusivity, the glass ceiling, the glass ladder, and the broken rungs, I'm beyond grateful for the few outstanding executive leaders who served as mentors, sponsors, and champions for my professional growth. Honorable Quinton Lucas, Mayor of Kansas City, Missouri; Tim Youngblood, Former Chief Security Officer T-Mobile, India Boulton, Senior Vice President Legal Counsel, T-Mobile, Edwige Robinson, Former Senior Vice President, T-Mobile Engineering; Tim Rains, Vice President & Chief Information Security Officer, ADT Home Security, and Dr. Derald Davis, Deputy Superintendent for Kansas City Public Schools, thank you for seeing me, recognizing my talents, and being the wind beneath my wings when I needed it most. Each of you ensured I had a seat at the table so that my voice and diverse perspectives were heard and embraced. I wouldn't be where I am today without all of you.

To Jamal Tate with Tate Design Group, thank you for capturing the visual essence of my book. Your work truly reflects the spirit of my journey. I also want to thank my editor, Stephanie Johnson of BrandDNA Group, who helped me finalize my vision for the book. Your help in shaping my personal stories and messages uniquely and thoughtfully ensures that this book will forever serve as a written source of truth and proven strategies for women to thrive in tech and cybersecurity.

To everyone who has played a sacred role in helping me on this journey, thank you for your support, belief in me, and encouragement. This book is possible because of you.

FOREWORD

Imagine this: you've worked hard, mastered your craft, and dreamed of making an impact in the world of cybersecurity and technology. Yet, despite your skills, drive, and ambitions, the path ahead feels unclear, like a maze filled with invisible barriers and unspoken rules.

You're not alone. Many have stood at that same crossroads, feeling both the weight of possibility and the sting of uncertainty. The truth is, the rules of the game can often feel unclear, with obstacles that seem to favor some while keeping others at bay. But what if you could redefine the game? What if you could step onto the field and rise to dominate it?

That's where this book, *Breaking The Code: Winning Strategies for Women in Cybersecurity & Tech*, comes in. This is more than a guide; it's a lifeline, a map, and a source of empowerment for those ready to take control of their careers. It doesn't shy away from the realities of navigating an industry that sometimes feels isolating. Instead, it embraces the truth, equips you with tools, and lights the way forward.

This book is a resounding yes for every woman who wonders whether she belongs in this field. It reminds us that our unique perspective is not only valuable but vital. In cybersecurity, the very essence of innovation lies in diverse thought and collaborative solutions. Your voice is needed now more than ever.

The strategies and insights within these pages aren't just about overcoming obstacles; they're about owning your power, building support networks, and rewriting the narrative of what leadership in tech can look like. With every step you take, you're advancing your career and paving the way for those who will follow.

To industry leaders and allies, this book challenges creating spaces where talent is nurtured, equity is prioritized, and barriers are dismantled. The security of our digital future depends on our ability to build diverse, inclusive teams that reflect the world we protect.

To everyone reading this book, know that you are capable, powerful, and belong. The career you've dreamed of isn't just possible; it's waiting for you to claim it. Let this book be your guide, your inspiration, and your call to action.

The future of cybersecurity is evolving, and bold, brilliant minds like yours are shaping it. The challenges may be real, but so is your ability to overcome them. With the strategies in this book, you're not just playing the game; you're rewriting the rules and claiming your place as a leader. The time is now. Let's make it happen!

Edwige A. Robinson

Forbes Tech Council Member | Senior Executive & Board Member | Author | Speaker | Trailblazer

INTRODUCTION

BREAKING

THE CODE OF SILENCE

A silent crisis is unfolding in our modern world's vast digital landscape. Despite the growing importance of cybersecurity in safeguarding our digital assets and infrastructure, the field grapples with a glaring issue: a startling lack of diversity and inclusion of people and perspectives. This disparity is particularly pronounced for all women, especially women of color and minorities, which means the cybersecurity workforce tasked with protecting our most sensitive personal information and systems does not reflect the diverse society it serves.

Women, who comprise 51% of the population, represent only 24% of cybersecurity professionals. The numbers are even more dismal for ethnic and racial minorities, who account for approximately 26% of the industry's workforce.

But these aren't just statistics. They represent missed opportunities, untapped innovations, and perspectives that could be pivotal in combating the ever-evolving cyber threats our nation faces. As we stand on the brink of a new era of technology defined by automation, quantum computing, and artificial intelligence, the need for diverse minds in tech and cybersecurity has never been more critical. The lack of diversity in these fields has far-reaching implications that extend well beyond the realms of fairness and equal opportunity. In a space where anticipating and outmaneuvering adversaries is paramount, homogeneity of thought and experience is a critical vulnerability. Each unique perspective brings the potential for innovative solutions and problem-solving approaches. Most importantly, it provides a deeper understanding of the diverse user base we aim to protect. With cybersecurity threats as diverse as our global population, shouldn't our defenses be equally multifaceted?

To give you a better perspective, let me take you back to a time when the world was far from the sleek, humming server rooms of today's tech industry.

Picture this: Kansas City in the late '70s, when the air was often thick with the aroma of home-cooked meals. It was a time when kiddos played outdoors in the neighborhood until the streetlights came on and drank water from fire hydrants on hot summer days. It was a time when Kool-Aid was the preferred drink of choice, and playing kickball or baseball in the streets to the metallic clang of bats hitting the ball was how we socialized. This was my childhood. The internet and social media were unheard of back then, and TV offered a grand total of five channels.

But don't let the seemingly idyllic scene I describe fool you. My neighborhood was far from perfect. Drugs and violence lurked in the shadows, government aid and food stamps were commonplace, and the scars of institutionalized segregation ran deep. My high school had exactly one white student, a stark reminder of the racial divide that defined the reality of Black and Brown people in America. Still, as challenging as it was, my environment became the crucible from which my resilience and determination were forged. Growing up, I made choices that weren't always in my best interest. But I refused to let my zip code dictate my future. I had an unshakable stubborn determination that helped transform me from little Cheryl, who grew up in the hood, to Dr. Cheryl Cooper.

Today, I am a professional titan who didn't just survive her childhood environment but galvanized the strength to thrive despite it. My journey to success isn't just about the fact that I overcame crippling circumstances and systemic barriers; it's about my audacity to succeed in a world seemingly hell-bent on holding me back.

As a Black woman, a "brown sugar queen," if you will, the color of my skin has been my most powerful motivator but also my heaviest burden. Yet, being discriminated against based on the hue of my skin somehow pushed me to silence the haters, dismiss any doubts, and soar far beyond the violent streets of Kansas City, where I grew up. I now think of my skin color and womanhood as my twin superpowers. They are the two reasons that propelled me to sign up to serve in the United States Navy, where I first fell in love with technology.

What I didn't know back then is that neither my skin color nor my womanhood would prepare me for the barrage of obstacles that lay ahead in my life: A minefield of sexism, racism, and colorism that often left me feeling as invisible as the tech bits and bytes I was learning about as an enlisted Petty Officer Second Class in the Navy.

It didn't take me long to realize that the tech world was not designed with someone like me in mind. Every day was a battle to excel and be seen, heard, and recognized for my contributions. Towards the end of my second tour in the Navy, I experienced a traumatic event that left me struggling with Post Traumatic Stress Disorder (PTSD), a mental health condition caused by a highly stressful or terrifying event-either being part of it or witnessing it. Struggling with the symptoms of PTSD while simultaneously trying to gain my sea legs in the tech and Cybersecurity world was complicated. Seeking help to overcome my condition became a personal battle but a crucial step on my journey toward healing and empowerment. The stigma surrounding mental health, particularly in the Black community and military, added an extra layer of complexity to my recovery. Through it all, I learned there is tremendous power in being vulnerable, getting professional help, and breaking the stigmas often associated with mental health and trauma in diverse communities.

I wouldn't be where I am today, recognized as a national tech and Cybersecurity Thought Leader and mentor, had it not been for my life experiences, both the triumphs and the adversities. My diversity and our diversity as a nation make us all unique, which is why I am compelled to highlight the critical importance of ensuring more diversity and inclusion within the tech and cybersecurity industry. I've seen firsthand how diverse teams can approach problems from multiple angles, creating and contributing to more robust and innovative solutions. I've also witnessed the transformative power of representation. There is nothing quite like the magic you feel when you see a spark in a young Black girl's eyes when she encounters someone who looks like her in a role that she dreams of holding someday. A woman in her hue who has already traveled the road she is eager to embark upon and who has already created a roadmap for her to follow.

My journey into tech and cybersecurity was far from straightforward. Although I had a background in information technology and computer networks, I lacked guidance and mentorship, particularly from individuals who looked like me. This made my transition into cybersecurity longer and more challenging than necessary.

But here's the thing: every obstacle, setback, and moment of doubt has led me to this moment—to this book—to you. This book isn't just my story. It's an invitation to join forces, lift each other, and cultivate courage, resilience, and sisterhood. It's a call to action to reshape and transform the tech and cybersecurity industries from the inside out.

Whether you're a seasoned cybersecurity professional, an aspiring entrant to the field, or simply someone who recognizes the critical role of diversity in shaping our digital future, this book offers a wealth of resources and insights, including:

1. A detailed guide for cybersecurity beginners that simplifies technical jargon clarifies complex concepts, and outlines a clear progression from entry-level roles to leadership positions.

2. Step-by-step instructions for newcomers on setting up a home computer lab for cybersecurity work. You don't need a state-of-the-art lab to get started. You'll learn how to create a robust learning environment with the resources you already have available.

3. Practical strategies for women navigating corporate America include addressing common challenges such as imposter syndrome, confidence building, and overcoming promotion barriers.

4. Targeted advice and actionable steps for women of color on dealing with microaggressions, tokenism, and the "double bind" of being both a woman and a person of color in a predominantly white male field.

5. Emerging trends, growth opportunities, and specializations where diverse perspectives are particularly valuable.

6. Real-life stories of resilience and success from women who have broken barriers, shattered glass ceilings, and paved the way for others in the field.

7. Strategies for creating a more inclusive and innovative tech and cybersecurity landscape from education and recruitment to retention and leadership development.

This book will guide you through the complex world of tech and cybersecurity. It provides clear, accessible explanations of key concepts, practical advice on beginning your journey, and a list of roles that best suit your skills and interests.

Through the lens of my experiences and those of other successful women in the field, you will gain valuable insights to help you chart your path to leadership and uncover why mentorship, sponsorship, and leveraging professional relationships are critical to your success.

We all have defining moments in our lives, crossroads where we're forced to make a choice that will alter our path forever. I hope reading this book will be one of those moments for you. Of course, reshaping the tech and cybersecurity industry to be more inclusive and equitable won't happen overnight. It will require harnessing the power of our collective efforts, one bit, one byte, and one brilliant mind at a time.

As we embark on this journey together, remember that your unique experiences, perspectives, and insights are invaluable assets in tech and cybersecurity. Your voice matters, your contributions are needed, and your presence in this field is essential.

Call to Action: Are you ready? You are part of the tech and cybersecurity evolution. The moment you decided to pursue your passion for technology despite the obstacles, you joined the ranks of those already challenging the status quo and breaking down barriers to create a cybersecurity landscape that truly reflects and protects our diverse world.

TABLE OF CONTENTS

CHAPTER ONE

THE BINARY BATTLEFIELD

"Diversity is not just a moral imperative; it's a strategic advantage in the fight against cyber threats."

~ *Unknown*

Welcome to the binary battlefield, where the stark underrepresentation of women in cybersecurity and technology roles is not just a footnote but a headline. It is a critical vulnerability that demands immediate attention. In this chapter, we'll explore women's multifaceted challenges in the tech industry and the urgent need for change. I propose that this issue isn't merely a diversity matter; it's a security threat that impacts the very fabric of our digital defenses.

Current statistics paint a sobering picture for women. It's as if we're running a system with only a quarter of its processing power. Women hold only 26% of computing jobs in the broader technology sector. And the numbers don't get better as women climb the tech corporate ladder. Instead, they dwindle like data packets lost in transmission, with only 18% of women serving as chief information officers or chief technology officers. The tech industry has a leaky talent pipeline at every level, and by the time women reach the top, it's barely a trickle. For women of color, the statistics are even more grim. Black women make up only 3% of the computing and information sciences workforce, while Hispanic women account for just 1%.

Diversity Matters

Diversity matters because underrepresentation is a security issue. Building a robust network with only a handful of nodes is impossible. Cybersecurity, at its core, is about protecting against threats. But how can we effectively defend against diverse threats if our defenders all look and think alike? It's like trying to create a comprehensive antivirus program using only a single type of malware for testing. The system is putting us at risk.

As cyber-attacks increase in size, scale, and sophistication, the global demand for cybersecurity professionals continues to skyrocket across all sectors. Yet, the supply of qualified professionals can't keep pace, resulting in a staggering 3.5 million unfilled cyber jobs globally, with half a million of these jobs vacant in the United States (U.S.) alone. Every unfilled position represents a potential vulnerability in our digital defenses.

The lack of diversity in cybersecurity further compounds the U.S. talent shortage. Women in cybersecurity often face formidable barriers, including gender bias, a lack of mentorship, and limited access to professional development opportunities. One study by the Aspen Institute found that women in cybersecurity roles are more likely to feel undervalued, pass over for promotions, and typically leave the field mid-career compared to their male counterparts. Underrepresentation stifles innovation and perpetuates an unwelcoming and discouraging culture for aspiring female cybersecurity professionals.

By failing to tap into the full potential of women and minorities, we're creating an open port in our defenses, leaving organizations more vulnerable to attacks. The underrepresentation of women in tech and cybersecurity also has significant economic implications. Studies have shown that companies with more diverse teams that include women also perform better financially. To put it bluntly, the industry is not just missing out on great, diverse talent but on new potential breakthroughs.

Bias in Technology: A Personal Anecdote

Let me share a personal story that illustrates the real-world impact of underrepresentation. A few years ago, I was part of a team developing a new intrusion detection system. During the testing phase, we discovered the system had a higher false positive rate for certain types of user behavior. As the team delved deeper, we realized these behaviors were more common amongst female users. Essentially, the all-male development team had unintentionally built their own biases into the system. To say the least, the entire experience was a wake-up call for all of us, but especially me. As a leader and woman of color, it reaffirmed my position that having more diverse teams that include women will

3

ensure we build more essential and effective security solutions for everyone.

The Educational Pipeline

The reasons behind women's underrepresentation in tech and cybersecurity are complex and multifaceted. They range from educational pipeline issues, with fewer women pursuing STEM degrees, to workplace culture problems that push women out of the field mid-career. Women of color represent the most significant minority in STEM fields, with only 3% of Black women and 4% of Latina women earning doctorate degrees. Only 1 out of every 20 employed scientists or engineers are women of color. Some scholars have argued that the widespread belief that cybersecurity is more suited to males is another significant factor. It's a self-fulfilling prophecy; the industry's lack of visible female role models discourages young women from entering the field. This leads to fewer role models, which, in turn, exacerbates the reluctance of women to pursue careers in tech, cybersecurity, and so on. It's an unfortunate cycle that we need to break.

It also doesn't help that many secondary schools nationwide don't encourage young girls to pursue interests in science and technology. Instead, girls may be steered towards the humanities or social sciences, while boys are encouraged to pursue math and science. Early-stage discouragement within the school system often stems from deep-seated stereotypes about gender roles, which has lasting ripple effects, including fewer women enrolling in computer science and engineering programs when they enter college.

Workplace Culture and Retention

Women continue to face barriers as they begin their tech or cybersecurity careers. Both industries have long been criticized for their "bro cultures," which can feel very unwelcoming to women as they try to adapt to workplace cultures not designed to foster their retention or advancement.

The challenges that come with trying to connect with male colleagues who don't share your experiences or perspectives while at the same time enduring microaggressions, discrimination, and even harassment have had a significant impact on women remaining in the field and advancing in tech and cybersecurity careers.

The "Broken Rung" Phenomenon

Another critical issue is the "broken rung" phenomenon. Research shows that women in tech and cybersecurity are less likely to be promoted to the crucial first step in leadership and management. For every 100 men promoted to a manager position, only 86 women receive the same opportunity. This disparity impacts representation at every subsequent level of leadership. The challenges are even more pronounced for women of color, who often face the double burden of gender and racial bias, which means they are more likely to feel isolated in the workplace because of the lack of access to influential leadership mentors or sponsors who look like them.

The "broken rung" phenomenon highlights the systemic barriers that prevent women from advancing in their careers. These include biased performance evaluations, lack of access to high-visibility projects, and limited opportunities for leadership development. Addressing these barriers will require a multi-pronged approach and a concerted collective effort across multiple sectors to drive change and create a more equitable support system and promotional infrastructure for women in the workplace.

The Impact of Implicit Bias

Implicit bias also plays a significant role in the underrepresentation of women in cybersecurity. Implicit biases are unconscious attitudes or stereotypes that affect our understanding, actions, and decisions. In the tech industry, implicit biases can manifest in various ways. For example, women may be perceived as less competent in technical roles, leading to fewer opportunities for advancement. Implicit biases can also affect hiring decisions, with women being overlooked for positions in favor of less qualified male candidates. These biases will remain an obstacle until organizations implement consistent and continuous training programs that create a universal workplace culture of awareness and accountability.

It's time to rewrite the tech and cybersecurity industry code and debug the system that has for too long undervalued and underutilized the talents of women, especially women of color. I believe a concerted effort is needed to build confidence in women already working in tech and cybersecurity and those just entering the field. Even though it can be challenging to sustain confidence in environments where you are underrepresented, women must feel empowered to advocate for their ideas and pursue more leadership opportunities.

One strategy for building confidence is to seek out mentors and sponsors who can provide professional guidance and help support your career growth. Ideally, mentors will provide invaluable insights on navigating workplace politics, while your sponsors will serve as personal career advancement advocates. The best Sponsors are willing to help you gain access to opportunities and roles that wouldn't ordinarily be within your reach. Additionally, women can benefit from professional development programs that enhance their leadership skills and self-advocacy. Every mentor voice that lifts you up, every new opportunity you gain with a sponsor's help, and every new professional development skill you learn provide a confidence booster that inoculates you from giving up and keeps you moving forward.

Finding Mentors and Advocating for Yourself

One approach to finding mentors is seeking them in professional organizations, networking events, and online tech and cybersecurity communities. These platforms provide opportunities to connect with diverse, experienced professionals who may be open to serving as career mentors. The value of having a trusted confidant and voice of reason you can readily reach out to for guidance and support as you navigate key decisions, challenges, and opportunities is truly priceless.

Another critical component of career advancement is learning how to advocate for yourself.

To be an effective self-advocate, you must spend time intensely focused on understanding and mastering your unique skills and strengths to communicate your values confidently. This involves identifying and documenting your accomplishments, including key projects, successful initiatives, and any positive feedback you've received. This information will ensure you are well-positioned to proactively discuss your career goals with your manager and seek new opportunities.

If you don't know where to start, you can seek feedback from current colleagues and your manager, who can help you identify areas where you shine and any areas for improvement. You can also reach out to individuals you regularly collaborate with from different departments or external peers who can give you valuable insights to increase your chances of getting noticed.

Women Who've Broken
the Glass Firewall Ceiling

Throughout the tech and cybersecurity industry, there are some inspiring examples of women who have broken through the glass firewall and achieved success. These women have overcome significant barriers and paved the way for future generations of female cybersecurity professionals.

I want to highlight two such examples: Parisa Tabriz and Ann Barron-DiCamillo. Parisa, fondly known in the cybersecurity world as Google's "Security Princess," has made significant contributions to the field of cybersecurity, including spearheading the team responsible for securing Google Chrome. Parisa faced numerous challenges and biases as a woman in a male-dominated field. However, her fierce determination, expertise, and leadership skills helped her overcome these barriers. She continues to advocate for diversity and inclusion in the tech industry, emphasizing the importance of diverse perspectives in solving complex security problems.

Parisha has also achieved highly visible accolades, such as being named among Forbes Magazine's Top "30 Under 30" in Technology and one of Wired's Top 20 Tech Visionaries. These awards have made her a sought-after industry Thought Leader who has inspired many women to pursue careers in tech and cybersecurity. Parisa's success demonstrates women's significant impact in the industry and serves as a shining example of women's contributions to help transform tech and cybersecurity as we advance.

Ann Barron-DiCamillo's distinguished career as the Chief of the Department of Homeland Security's U.S. Computer Emergency Readiness Team (US-CERT) is also known for breaking the glass ceiling in the cybersecurity industry. Her efforts at US-CERT helped to protect the nation's internet infrastructure from cyberattacks and data breaches, which were critical to fortifying the nation's cybersecurity defenses.

Ann's story is a powerful example of how determination, expertise, and advocacy can break down racial and gender barriers in the cybersecurity industry and lead to enormous success. As a diverse woman in a predominantly male field, she faced numerous challenges. However, undeterred, Ann continued to thrive by demonstrating exceptional leadership and technical skills, ultimately impacting the cybersecurity landscape. She, too, continues to be a strong advocate for the inclusion of women in the field, and her leadership, like Parisa's, is helping to close the gender gap and empower future generations of women cybersecurity professionals.

As we stand on the brink of a new era, the rapid advancement of technologies such as AI and quantum computing presents an opportunity to infuse diversity and inclusion into the foundation of these new fields. By prioritizing diversity from the outset, organizations will ensure the nation is well-positioned to create and elevate more effective solutions that address the needs of a diverse global population.

Companies can take several proven steps, including setting diversity targets, implementing more inclusive hiring practices, establishing leadership mentor programs for diverse hires, and fostering supportive, collaborative environments for underrepresented groups. Additionally, organizations can invest in providing continuous employee training on diversity and inclusion and develop programs that focus on building new diverse talent pipelines.

Social allies can also play a vital role in promoting more diversity and inclusion in tech and cybersecurity, using their platforms to support and amplify the voices of underrepresented groups. Influential Thought Leaders can use their positions of privilege to push for systemic changes that promote continued equity and inclusion in the industry. Regardless of what's happening in the backdrop of the country, companies should not retreat in the fight for inclusion. The underrepresentation of women and minorities in tech and cybersecurity represents a critical vulnerability within the system. But with the right tools, strategies, and mindset, it's a flaw we can fix.

Call to Action

You, too, can join the binary battlefield and commit to championing the transformation of the tech and cybersecurity landscape. This includes advocating for systemic change within your sphere of influence in support of women and minorities at every industry level, especially women of color. Whether you're a leader in the field or an aspiring tech or cybersecurity professional, your role in transformation is vital. Together, with diverse voices and perspectives at the table, future possibilities are endless.

CHAPTER TWO

CRACKING THE CODE: YOUR CYBERSECURITY JOURNEY BEGINS

"The journey of a thousand miles begins with a single step."

~Lao Tzu

Starting a new career can feel like being dropped into a maze without a map. I remember the early days of my career so vividly. Walking into a bustling office filled with buzzing conversations and the hum of computers, feeling both a sense of excitement and no direction. It was a brand-new culture of unspoken rules, office politics, and strategic maneuvers that seemed as complex as the lines of code scrolling across my screen. I quickly realized that an entire game was being played, which no one had taught me.

I stumbled upon figuring it out on my own through trial and error. Even when there were people around me who could help, I honestly didn't know what questions to ask them. It was as if I had stumbled upon a hidden language that everyone else around me could speak except me. So, whether you're fresh out of school or transitioning from another career, I understand how it feels to "go it alone" as a newbie and a diverse woman trying your best to decode the mysteries of a tech and cybersecurity culture that makes you feel you have no place or space to occupy. I hope my personal stories serve as a guide and spark to keep you going so you never give up on your dreams.

Igniting New Sparks

I remember the day like it was yesterday. A young woman approached me at a conference right after my session on the importance of diversity in cybersecurity. Her eyes were bright with curiosity, but there was also a hint of nervousness and uncertainty. "Dr. Cooper," she said, "I'm interested in a career in cybersecurity, but I have no idea where to start because it all seems so overwhelming."

I smiled, recognizing the same eagerness and trepidation I felt at the beginning of my journey. "Well," I replied. "You've already taken the first and most important step—deciding to do this. Now, let's talk about how to turn that spark into a flame."

Passion like this young lady's is valuable for the tech and cybersecurity industry and necessary.

The purpose of this chapter is two-fold. I want to empower you with new knowledge about how you can help encourage more young, diverse students to pursue careers in tech and cybersecurity. I also hope you gain valuable insights from my perspectives and experiences and to help you achieve a highly successful career.

Planting More Seeds of Curiosity

Perhaps one of the most crucial aspects of building a diverse cybersecurity workforce is engaging young people earlier in their educational journey. The earlier we can introduce these concepts, the better.

I remember being invited to teach at an inner-city school in Kansas City as part of an outreach program. The students, primarily girls from underrepresented communities, studied my every move when I entered the room. I will never forget their little faces filled with curiosity and skepticism as I set up my laptop and a small network of devices. "Today," I announced with a grin. "We're going to learn how to become ethical hackers." The room began buzzing with excitement. Over the next hour, we explored the basic concepts of network security, practiced some simple coding, and simulated a (very basic) cyber-attack. By the end of the session, any skepticism the young girls had at the outset of class had vanished. Instead, I witnessed the birth of wide-eyed enthusiasm. A seed had been planted.

One student, a young girl named Aisha, stayed behind after class. "Dr. Cooper," she said, her voice barely above a whisper. "I never knew computers could be so cool. Do you believe I could have a shot at this?" I looked straight into her big brown almond-shaped eyes and said, "Aisha, I don't just believe it. I know you can." I explained to Aisha that her unique talents and way of thinking would bring valuable contributions to the industry someday if she remained determined and never gave up."

That's the power of intentional early engagement. It's more than just teaching technical skills; it's a commitment to planting seeds of encouragement in young minds, especially those from underrepresented groups. Giving these children a real spark of curiosity and nurturing their passion into action ensures they fully understand their rich contributions to the tech industry and the world.

Bridging the Gap

Early engagement is only just the beginning. To truly build a diverse talent pipeline, the industry must also create sustainable educational outreach programs that provide resources, support, and opportunities for young minorities to explore and develop their interests in tech and cybersecurity regularly.

That's why organizations like Cyber Patriots are game changers—Cyber Patriots partners with inner-city schools to offer cybersecurity educational programs for young girls after school. I've had the privilege of hosting several workshops for Cyber Patriots over the years, and each time, the students were fully engrossed in the hands-on exercises that I prepared.

I recall giving the students one assignment that required them to work in small teams to identify vulnerabilities in a simulated network. The room was filled with the sounds of rapid typing as they attempted to uncover possible weaknesses in the system. One of the teams was led by a soft-spoken young lady named Maria, whose group found a particularly tricky vulnerability that even some of the more advanced students missed. When I asked Maria to explain how her team uncovered the vulnerability, she hesitated initially, but with encouragement, she soon lit up as she walked the class through their process. "I just thought about it differently," she said, her confidence growing with each word. "I put myself in the shoes of someone who might want to exploit the system, and then I encouraged the team to follow my thinking and look for the least obvious way in."

That moment stuck with me. It was a perfect example of why diversity in cybersecurity is so crucial. Maria's unique perspective allowed her to help her team approach the problem in a way that others hadn't considered.

Diverse viewpoints matter; I believe they are our secret weapon for staying ahead of future national and international cyber threats.

Benefits of Immersive Learnings

While after-school programs are great, students sometimes must dive deeper into more immersive environments to spark curiosity. That's where cybersecurity camps and workshops come in. These intensive, hands-on experiences can be transformative for young students interested in technology and cybersecurity.

Workshop series such as Girls in Cybersecurity (GIC) feel like experiencing the Superbowl in person. The touchdowns these young minds score while participating in structured workshops are breathtaking to watch and cheer on. One summer, I was tapped by GIC to help set up a challenge where the students had to work in small teams to find and exploit vulnerabilities in a simulated system. I'll never forget the sheer determination of one participant, Jasmine. She had been quiet most of the workshop, but something about this challenge fully energized her. She and her team worked tirelessly for hours, trying different approaches, collaborating, and problem-solving. When they finally cracked the challenge, the room erupted in cheers. Jasmine's face was beaming with pride as she high-fived her teammates. Later, she told me, "Dr. Cooper, I never knew I could do something like this. I always thought cybersecurity was for, you know, computer geniuses or something. But this... this feels like solving puzzles, and I love it!" That's the magic of immersive experiences. They allow adolescents to discover capabilities they never knew they had.

Tapping The Robust Talent Pool of HBCUs

Perhaps one of the most significant opportunities to build a more diverse tech and cybersecurity workforce is tapping the robust talent pool of Historically Black Colleges and Universities (HBCUs). These institutions have a long and proud history of preparing Black students for successful careers in STEM.

Being more deliberate about bringing together companies and HBCUs to build a pipeline of diverse talent is an ideal way to make great strides in increasing the number of diverse women and men who enter the tech and cybersecurity fields. Several industries are already successfully doing this, including the armed services, health and allied services, and many more. Through internships, scholarships, and joint research projects, students in their junior and senior years of college can get hands-on experience to ensure they are well-equipped to seamlessly transition into junior roles at businesses looking to diversify their talent pool and prepare for the next generation of leaders.

The Power of Mentorship

Now, let's discuss something incredibly close to my heart: mentorship. I firmly believe that behind every successful person in any field is a network of mentors who have guided, supported, and challenged them.

As president of the Women in CyberSecurity (WiCyS) Kansas City Metroplex, I've had the opportunity to mentor and be mentored by some incredible women in this field. And let me tell you, there's nothing quite like watching someone you've mentored grow and succeed in their career.

I remember a few years ago when one of my mentees, Sophia, came to me feeling stuck in her career. While Sophia had excellent technical skills, she struggled to advance and ensure her voice was heard amongst her male colleagues. Together, Sophia and I worked on developing her leadership skills to boost her confidence and explore ways she could begin asserting her voice more and stepping up for new, more significant projects. It wasn't always easy for Sophia. There were setbacks and moments of frustration. But she was determined, and her zeal eventually paid off. A few months after we got started, Sophia called me. Her voice was brimming with excitement. "Dr. Cooper, I did it! I just got promoted to lead my own security team."

We celebrated her success with cheers and prayers of thanks. But what really struck me was what Sophia said next. "You know, Dr. Cooper, I couldn't have done this without your support. And now, I'm paying it forward by mentoring a junior analyst on my team."

That's the beauty of mentorship: It creates a ripple effect. Every mentored person becomes empowered to mentor others, creating new networks of support connections that rewire the system and elevate the industry.

Addressing Unconscious Biases

Now, let's tackle a challenging but crucial topic: unconscious biases. These are hidden prejudices that can create significant barriers for women and people of color in cybersecurity, often in ways that are hard to identify and address.

Early in my career, I recall being one of only a handful of women and the only Black woman in attendance at a mid-size cybersecurity conference. During one of the networking sessions, I approached a group of men discussing a new security protocol. I noticed their surprised looks as I joined the conversation and shared my thoughts. One even said, "Wow, you really know your stuff." While I'm sure he meant it as a compliment, it revealed an unconscious bias—the assumption that, as a Black woman, it was surprising that I was very knowledgeable about cybersecurity. Unconscious biases can have a real impact on hiring decisions, promotions, and day-to-day workplace interactions.

There is no way to address these deep-seated biases without committing to ongoing education, especially within corporate America. The truth is that while America is a melting pot, people tend to be very tribal in nature, which means we are linked by social, economic, religious, or blood ties with our shared culture and communities. Studies show that even in diverse public-school settings, groups of children are much more likely to bond with those who reflect their same hue, culture, and background.

This makes it virtually impossible for students to be free of unconscious biases about other race groups as they continue matriculating through college and into the workforce. As an industry leader, I've helped implement bias training programs for employee groups and organizations. These programs were critical in assisting individuals to recognize their biases and adopt strategies to mitigate biased behavior and actions.

One particularly effective exercise, "Flip It to Test It," presents participants with scenarios where they are asked to flip their gender or race with others in their assigned group. If they become extremely uncomfortable in the flipped gender or race role they are playing, unconscious bias likely exists. I've seen real, lasting change happen after exercises like this. I remember an IT manager approached me after participating in a Flip It to Test It session. He said, "Dr. Cooper, I had no idea I was carrying these biases. I will completely revamp our hiring process to make it fairer and more inclusive." This realization and personal accountability can transform our industry and create more opportunities for diverse talent to thrive in cybersecurity.

Navigating the Certification Landscape

One of the most significant advantages you can give yourself to others to overcome biases about you is the gift of earning additional degrees and certifications. As you embark on your cybersecurity journey, you'll quickly realize that certifications are crucial. They're like badges of honor, demonstrating your expertise and skills to potential employers. You're only lying to yourself if you believe educational pedigree and additional certifications don't give you a competitive advantage, especially if you are a minority. But with so many certifications out there, it can be overwhelming to know where to start. Let me share a little secret: not all certifications are created equal. Many eager newcomers waste time and money on advanced certifications before they're ready. Instead, I encourage you to focus on acquiring certifications that will give you a solid foundation in cybersecurity principles.

Certifications in cybersecurity principles will enhance your resume and expose you to real-world knowledge and experiences that can help you tackle challenges you will likely face in junior roles as you begin your career.

As you grow in your career, you can pursue more specialized certifications tailored to your interests, such as ethical hacking, network security, cybersecurity management, etc. Remember, it's not just about collecting certifications; it's about strategically gaining more profound practical knowledge to help guide your career decisions and ultimately help you achieve your goals.

Building a Career Community

Beyond certifications and technical skills, a supportive community is one of the most valuable assets you can cultivate in your cybersecurity career. This includes a network of peers, mentors, and colleagues who will serve as your "sounding boards," advisors, and cheerleaders as you navigate the challenges and triumphs of your career. It's easy to start immediately by attending conferences, joining professional organizations, and participating in online forums and discussion groups that share your passion for cybersecurity. As part of my journey, I've been fortunate to be a member of several vibrant communities that have supported and provided me with invaluable insights, encouragement, and opportunities for growth.

Staying Ahead of the Curve

Because the field of cybersecurity is ever-evolving, it's also essential to stay ahead of the curve. Technology is constantly changing, with new threats and challenges emerging every day. This requires a commitment to continuous learning and professional development to become a successful and sought-after thought leader. My personal and professional motto: If you are not learning, you are not growing. So, whether it's pursuing additional niche certifications or making sure you are regularly taking time out to be "In the Know" about the latest industry news and trends, lifelong learning is essential for maintaining your edge and ensuring that you stay on the cusp of innovation with an eye toward the future.

Remember, your journey in cybersecurity is not just about acquiring technical skills. It's about cracking the code of the professional world and finding your unique place within it. The world of cybersecurity is vast and ever-changing, and it needs voices like yours. As you move forward, embrace the challenges and opportunities that come your way. Stay curious, stay determined, and, most importantly, stay true to yourself.

CHAPTER THREE

CHARTING YOUR COURSE: NAVIGATING THE CYBER SECURITY SEAS

"The future belongs to those who believe in the beauty of their dreams."

~Eleanor Roosevelt

Looking back on my career, I often find myself standing at the edge of a vast ocean, each wave representing a different experience, challenge, or lesson learned. The journey through cybersecurity has been anything but linear. I've encountered many twists and turns that felt like navigating a ship through unpredictable waters. Every role I've had throughout my career has shaped my understanding that tech and cybersecurity offer a world brimming with opportunities and adventures waiting to be explored.

In this chapter, I'll go deep into the various career paths you can chart in the cybersecurity industry, including day-to-day responsibilities and what skills are needed to succeed. When you graduate from college, you have a blank passport to go wherever your heart desires within tech and cybersecurity. Think of it as embarking upon a new journey filled with self-discovery as you uncover the unique path awaiting you.

A World of Possibilities

Imagine standing at the helm of a ship, gazing out at a vast tech and cybersecurity ocean. In every direction, islands of opportunity await, each representing a different specialization or role. With that in mind, let's set sail and explore the possibilities.

The Guardian of the Gates

Our first stop is the bustling port of Security Analysis, where vigilant guardians monitor the digital shores, ever watchful for signs of intrusion or attack. I remember my first job as a Security Analyst, the thrill of each shift as I settled into my chair, ready to confront whatever new horizons the day might bring.

A typical day as a Security Analyst begins with reviewing the latest threat intelligence reports. It's akin to reading a weather forecast; instead of predictions of rain or shine, you're looking for malware storm clouds or suspicious network activity.

From there, most of your day is spent monitoring network traffic, analyzing logs, and investigating alerts. This role demands a keen eye for detail and the ability to think critically under pressure, like an air traffic controller. There will be times when things run smoothly, and then there are the days when you may notice unusual patterns of data exfiltration. These days are filled with a utopic-like adrenaline rush as you partner with your colleagues to identify potential compromises within the system and contain any threats. Moments like these remind you of security analysts' vital role in safeguarding an organization's digital assets.

The Digital Sherlock Holmes: Penetration Testers

Next, we sail to the island of Penetration Testing, where modern-day Sherlock Holmes-like cybersecurity experts work tirelessly to uncover vulnerabilities before malicious actors can exploit them. Penetration Testers, also known as ethical hackers, serve as detectives in the cybersecurity realm. Their work is thrilling and essential. They meticulously plan and execute simulated attacks, documenting their findings to help organizations strengthen their cybersecurity defenses. It's like being paid to solve complex puzzles while making the digital world safer.

Maria, The Digital Sherlock Holmes

A Penetration Tester I once worked with, Maria, helped uncover a critical vulnerability in a major financial institution's mobile app. Her discovery potentially saved the company millions of dollars. It also helped to protect countless customers from having their data compromised. Maria is one of the most patient people I've ever met, which is why she was an excellent Penetration Tester. Her role requires enormous patience and a keen eye for detail. If you like diving into seemingly unsolvable puzzles to find the pieces that match or don't, you will do well in this essential position. Penetration Testers are vital to keeping hackers out of the systems of corporations that house your essential data.

The Digital Architect: The Security Engineers

Continuing our journey, we arrive at the towering citadel of Security Engineering. Here, skilled architects design and implement the very foundations of cybersecurity defenses.

Security Engineers are the masterminds behind firewalls, intrusion detection systems, and other security controls that keep our digital world safe. They are responsible for designing, implementing, and maintaining security measures that protect computer systems, networks, and data. Their ability to translate complex security requirements into robust technical solutions amazes me. In addition to configuring firewalls and updating company security protocols, Security Engineers ensure the posture of organizations is as strong as possible.

As a Security Engineer, you must be able to work across multiple business units within an organization to ensure security protocols are user-friendly and foster robust, widespread adoption. Successful Security Engineers bring a unique blend of technical expertise and practical problem-solving that makes them indispensable. This position requires a deep understanding of cybersecurity principles, threat modeling, and risk management.

Security Engineer Qualifications

- Educational Background: A Bachelor's Degree in Computer Science, Information Technology, Cybersecurity, or a related field is typically required.

Advanced degrees or certifications in cybersecurity (e.g., CISSP, CEH, CISM) are highly desirable.

- Technical Skills: Proficiency in various programming languages (e.g., Python, Java, C++), knowledge of operating systems (e.g., Windows, Linux), and experience with security tools and technologies (e.g., firewalls, intrusion detection systems, encryption).

- Analytical Skills: Strong problem-solving abilities and the ability to analyze complex security issues and develop practical solutions.

- Communication Skills: Excellent written and verbal communication skills to effectively convey security concepts to both technical and non-technical stakeholders.

- Certifications: Industry-recognized certifications such as Certified Information Systems Security Professional (CISSP), Certified Ethical Hacker (CEH), Certified Information Security Manager (CISM), and others.

Years of Experience

- Entry-Level: 0-2 years of experience in IT or cybersecurity roles. Entry-level Security Engineers often start with internships or junior positions to gain practical experience.

- Mid-Level: 3-5 years of experience in cybersecurity, with a proven track record of implementing security measures and responding to security incidents.

- Senior-Level: 6+ years of cybersecurity experience, extensive knowledge of security architecture, risk management, and leadership in security projects. Senior

Security Engineers often mentor junior staff and lead security initiatives within the organization.

Key Responsibilities

- Designing and implementing security measures to protect systems and data.

- Conducting vulnerability assessments and penetration testing.

- Monitoring and responding to security incidents and breaches.

- Collaborating with IT teams to integrate security protocols into all aspects of technology infrastructure.

- Staying up-to-date with the latest cybersecurity trends and threats.

The Digital Firefighter: The Incident Responder

Next is the high-stakes world of Incident Response. In cybersecurity, Incident Responders are like firefighters, rushing in when a breach is ablaze to contain the damage and extinguish the threat.

Choosing the career path of an Incident Responder is not for the faint of heart. These professionals must be able to think quickly and strategically during high-pressure situations while simultaneously

coordinating with multiple teams to mitigate the impact of a cyber-attack.

Incident Responders typically serve on the organization's Incident Response team. Their workload and visibility within the organization can ramp up quickly, sometimes requiring them to work around the clock and coordinate with IT, legal, and executive teams to contain a cybersecurity breach. If you desire to pursue a career as an Incident Responder, companies typically assess your unique skills, years of experience, and any special certifications you hold.

Special Skills

- Analytical Thinking: Ability to analyze and respond to security incidents quickly and effectively.

- Technical Proficiency: Knowledge of various operating systems, network protocols, and cybersecurity tools.

- Communication: Strong verbal and written communication skills to document incidents and communicate with stakeholders.

- Problem-Solving: Ability to identify the root cause of incidents and develop practical solutions.

Years of Experience

- Entry-Level: 0-2 years of experience in IT or cybersecurity roles, with a focus on incident response.

- Mid-Level: 3-5 years of experience in incident response or related cybersecurity roles.

- Senior-Level: 6+ years of experience in incident response, with a proven track record of handling complex security incidents.

Certifications

Certified Information Systems Security Professional (CISSP)

- Certified Incident Handler (GCIH)

- Certified Information Security Manager (CISM)

- Certified Ethical Hacker (CEH)

The Orchestrator: The Security Project Manager

As we continue navigating the complex waters of cybersecurity, we encounter the crucial role of the Security Project Manager. These professionals are the conductors of the cybersecurity orchestra, ensuring all security initiatives come together in harmony.

I've worked with exceptional Security Project Managers, and their ability to juggle multiple tasks, timelines, and stakeholders is remarkable. They take high-level security strategies developed by CISOs and turn them into actionable projects with clear milestones.

Sarah, The Orchestrator

I remember collaborating with a Project Manager, Sarah, on a large-scale security infrastructure upgrade. The project involved multiple teams, tight deadlines, and numerous technical challenges. Sarah's coordination of all moving parts and her ability to manage expectations aligned us toward our common goals. When we hit a significant roadblock, Sarah quickly organized a war room, bringing key players together for a problem-solving session that resolved the issue and improved our overall approach. Her calm demeanor and knack for drawing out the best in her team made all the difference. If you are considering a role as a Security Project Manager, you must have exceptional business acumen, problem-solving, superb communications skills, and strong project management experience. These combined skill sets will ensure you succeed as a Project Manager but are well-positioned to advance into leadership positions.

Risk Navigators: Governance, Risk, & Compliance Analysts

There will be times when you encounter treacherous waters as you sail the sea of cybersecurity. This is when having the proper Governance, Risk, and Compliance (GRC) Analysts on board is essential. GRC Analysts help organizations navigate regulatory requirements and compliance challenges.

They ensure security practices align with industry standards and legal requirements while managing the company's security risk protocols and procedures.

Michael, The Risk Navigator

I recall a challenging time when one of the organizations where I worked was preparing for a major compliance audit. Our GRC Analyst, Michael, was tasked with meticulously reviewing our security policies to identify compliance gaps and map out a plan to address them. His ability to translate complex regulatory requirements into actionable steps for our technical teams was impressive and helped ensure a smooth auditing process. If you desire to be a GRC Analyst, the following skills will serve you well.

Qualifications

- Educational Background: A Bachelor's Degree in Information Technology, Cybersecurity, Business Administration, or a related field is typically required. Advanced degrees in these areas are advantageous.

- Technical Knowledge: Understanding of IT systems, cybersecurity principles, and regulatory requirements.

Certifications

- Certified Information Systems Auditor (CISA)
- Certified in Risk and Information Systems Control (CRISC)
- Certified Information Systems Security Professional (CISSP)
- Certified Information Security Manager (CISM)

Special Skills

- Analytical Skills: Ability to assess risks, analyze data, and develop mitigation strategies.
- Communication: Strong verbal and written communication skills to effectively convey compliance requirements and risk assessments to stakeholders.
- Attention to Detail: Meticulous attention to detail to ensure compliance with regulations and standards.
- Problem-Solving: Ability to identify potential risks and develop effective solutions.
- Project Management: Skills in managing compliance projects and initiatives.

Years of Experience

- Entry-Level: 0-2 years of experience in IT, cybersecurity, or compliance roles.

- Mid-Level: 3-5 years of experience in governance, risk management, or compliance, with a proven track record of implementing GRC frameworks.

- Senior-Level: 6+ years of experience in GRC roles, with extensive knowledge of regulatory requirements and experience in leading compliance initiatives.

The Wise Counsel: The Security Consultant

As we sail on, we reach the island of Security Consulting, where seasoned professionals guide organizations through the complex waters of cybersecurity. Security Consultants are like the wise elders of our field, drawing on their vast experience to provide strategic advice.

As a seasoned Security Consultant, I've worked with various organizations, from small startups to large corporations. Each engagement presents unique challenges and learning opportunities. One day, I may conduct a risk assessment for a financial institution, while the next, I may be helping a tech startup develop its first comprehensive security policy.

I truly love that no two days are exactly the same and that I work with many different companies, including for-profit and non-profit organizations. Each engagement is unique, and although the projects and outcomes differ, the results are impactful.

I recall being tapped to help a non-profit organization struggling to secure donor data. Together, we developed a cost-effective security strategy that protected sensitive information and built more trust with donors. When I see the tangible impact of my work, moments like these make consulting such a rewarding career path. If being a consultant is desirable to you, it typically requires advanced degrees to be successful, a bevy of certifications, strong leadership skills, and extensive work experience in the industry.

Qualifications

- Educational Background: A Bachelor's Degree in Computer Science, Information Technology, Cybersecurity, or a related field is typically required. Advanced degrees in these areas are advantageous.

- Technical Knowledge: In-depth understanding of cybersecurity principles, threat modeling, risk management, and security frameworks.

Certifications

- Certified Information Systems Security Professional (CISSP)

- Certified Ethical Hacker (CEH)

- Certified Information Security Manager (CISM)

- Certified Information Systems Auditor (CISA)

- Certified in Risk and Information Systems Control (CRISC)

Special Skills

- Technical Proficiency: Expertise in various operating systems, network protocols, and cybersecurity tools.

- Analytical Thinking: Strong problem-solving skills and the ability to analyze complex security issues.

- Communication: Excellent written and verbal communication skills to effectively convey security concepts to both technical and non-technical stakeholders.

- Project Management: Skills in managing security projects and initiatives.

- Adaptability: Ability to stay updated with the latest cybersecurity trends and threats.

Years of Experience

- Entry-Level: 0-2 years of experience in IT or cybersecurity roles, focusing on security analysis and incident response.

- Mid-Level: 3-5 years of experience in cybersecurity consulting or related roles, with a proven track record of implementing security measures and responding to security incidents.

- Senior-Level: 6+ years of experience in cybersecurity consulting, with extensive knowledge of security architecture, risk management, and leadership in security projects. Senior consultants often mentor junior staff and lead security initiatives within the organization.

Captain of the Ship: The Chief Information Security Officer (CISO)

The Chief Information Security Officer (CISO) role is at the pinnacle of our cybersecurity journey. The CISO steers the cybersecurity ship, charting the course through calm and stormy seas.

As a CISO, you're responsible for developing and implementing an organization's overall information security strategy. This role requires a unique blend of technical knowledge, business acumen, and leadership skills. You must be able to communicate detailed security concepts to non-technical executives, make high-stakes decisions about risk management, and lead diverse teams. I've had the privilege of working with exceptional CISOs throughout my career. Their ability to navigate the complex landscape of cybersecurity while balancing business needs is remarkable.

A successful CISO can lead the organization through the constant evolution of digital transformation while ensuring security is maintained and integrated into every aspect of new system upgrades and industry changes. While there are many exceptional male CISOs out there, I've also had the privilege of serving alongside women CISOs whose diverse perspectives and visions have helped improve the security posture of the organizations and companies they have served and drive continuous innovation. Below are the ideal qualifications, certifications, and skills needed to become a CISO.

Qualifications

- Educational Background: A Bachelor's Degree in Computer Science, Information Technology, Cybersecurity, or a related field is typically required. Many CISOs also hold advanced degrees, such as a Master's in Business Administration (MBA) or Information Security.

- Technical Knowledge: Extensive understanding of cybersecurity principles, risk management, and security frameworks. Knowledge of regulatory requirements and industry standards is essential.

Certifications

- Certified Information Systems Security Professional (CISSP)

- Certified Information Security Manager (CISM)

- Certified Information Systems Auditor (CISA)

- Certified in Risk and Information Systems Control (CRISC)

- Certified Chief Information Security Officer (CCISO)

Special Skills

- Leadership: Strong leadership and management skills to lead security teams and initiatives.

- Strategic Thinking: Ability to develop and implement comprehensive security strategies aligned with business goals.

- Communication: Excellent written and verbal communication skills to effectively convey security concepts to technical and non-technical stakeholders, including executive leadership and board members.

- Risk Management: Expertise in identifying, assessing, and mitigating security risks.

- Problem-Solving: Strong analytical and problem-solving abilities to address complex security challenges.

- Project Management: Skills in managing large-scale security projects and initiatives.

Years of Experience

- Mid-Level: 5-7 years of experience in cybersecurity roles, with a focus on security management and leadership.

- Senior-Level: 8+ years of cybersecurity experience, extensive knowledge of security architecture, risk management, and leadership in security projects. Senior CISOs often have experience in executive roles and a proven track record of leading security initiatives within large organizations.

The Digital Detective: The Forensics Analyst

Navigating the ocean of cybersecurity requires an excellent Forensic Analyst. These digital detectives investigate cybercrimes and gather digital evidence to help unravel data breaches and much more. I once witnessed a Forensics Analyst solve a case of intellectual property theft by meticulously piecing together gigabytes of data to recover stolen property, ultimately leading to the perpetrators' prosecution. If you want to become a Forensic Analyst, companies will look for the right mix of educational pedigree, certifications, and special skills.

Qualifications

- Educational Background: A Bachelor's Degree in Computer Science, Information Technology, Cybersecurity, or a related field is typically required. Advanced degrees in Digital Forensics or Cybersecurity are advantageous.

- Technical Knowledge: In-depth understanding of digital forensics principles, methodologies, and tools.

Certifications

- Certified Computer Examiner (CCE)
- Certified Forensic Computer Examiner (CFCE)

- GIAC Certified Forensic Analyst (GCFA)
- Certified Information Systems Security Professional (CISSP)
- Certified Information Systems Auditor (CISA)

Special Skills

- Technical Proficiency: Expertise in various operating systems, file systems, and forensic tools (e.g., EnCase, FTK, X-Ways).

- Analytical Thinking: Strong problem-solving abilities and the capability to analyze complex digital evidence.

- Attention to Detail: Meticulous attention to detail ensures forensic investigations' accuracy and integrity.

- Communication: Excellent written and verbal communication skills to effectively document and present findings to stakeholders, including legal teams.

- Legal Knowledge: Understanding of legal and regulatory requirements related to digital forensics and evidence handling.

Years of Experience

- Entry-Level: 0-2 years of experience in IT, cybersecurity, or digital forensics roles.

- Mid-Level: 3-5 years of experience in digital forensics, with a proven track record of conducting forensic investigations and analyzing digital evidence.

- Senior-Level: 6+ years of experience in digital forensics, with extensive knowledge of forensic methodologies, tools, and leadership in forensic investigations. Senior Forensics Analysts often mentor junior staff and lead complex forensic projects.

The Code Keeper: The Cryptographer

A Cryptographer serves as the Cybersecurity Code Keeper, developing encryption algorithms to help safeguard data.

Throughout my career, I've known and collaborated with some brilliant cryptographers, one of whom created a novel encryption method that significantly enhanced the security of a well-known and well-used messaging app. Cryptographers require unique qualifications and skills, which is why the role is always in high demand.

Qualifications

- Educational Background: A Bachelor's Degree in Computer Science, Mathematics, Information Technology, or a related field is typically required. Advanced degrees in Cryptography, Mathematics, or Cybersecurity are highly advantageous.

- Technical Knowledge: In-depth understanding of cryptographic principles, algorithms, and protocols.

Certifications

- Certified Information Systems Security Professional (CISSP)

- Certified Encryption Specialist (EC-Council)

- Certified Information Security Manager (CISM)

- Certified Information Systems Auditor (CISA)

- Certified in Risk and Information Systems Control (CRISC)

Special Skills

- Mathematical Proficiency: Strong mathematical skills, particularly in number theory, algebra, and probability.

- Technical Proficiency: Expertise in various cryptographic algorithms and protocols (e.g., RSA, AES, ECC).

- Analytical Thinking: Strong problem-solving skills and the ability to analyze complex cryptographic systems.

- Attention to Detail: Meticulous attention to detail to ensure the accuracy and security of cryptographic implementations.

- Communication: Excellent written and verbal communication skills to effectively convey cryptographic concepts to technical and non-technical stakeholders.

- Programming Skills: Proficiency in programming languages such as Python, C++, and Java.

Years of Experience

- Entry-Level: 0-2 years of experience in IT, cybersecurity, or cryptography roles.

- Mid-Level: 3-5 years of experience in cryptography, with a proven track record of implementing cryptographic solutions and analyzing cryptographic systems.

- Senior-Level: 6+ years of experience in cryptography, with extensive knowledge of cryptographic algorithms, protocols, and leadership in cryptographic projects. Senior Cryptographers often mentor junior staff and lead complex cryptographic initiatives.

Beyond these specialized leadership roles, there are numerous other fields to consider. Each specialty is like its own unique island within a digital archipelago. Let's briefly touch on a few more:

The Oracle: The Threat Intelligence Analyst: Researches and analyzes emerging threats, providing insights to help organizations stay ahead. I remember one analyst who identified a new malware weeks before it spread, which helped the company implement vital preventive measures.

The Cloud Guardian: The Cloud Security Specialist: Focuses on securing cloud-based systems. I've seen Cloud Security Specialists develop comprehensive cloud security strategies for large e-commerce companies, ensuring customer data protection during rapid scaling.

The Code Protector: The Application Security Engineer: Works to ensure software applications are secure from the ground up. I've collaborated with engineers who implemented secure coding frameworks that reduce vulnerabilities and drive innovation.

The AI Guardian: The AI Security Specialist: Emerging new roles like this work to address security challenges posed by AI and machine learning systems.

The IoT Protector: The IoT Security Expert: Secures Internet of Things devices, preventing them from becoming cyberattack entry points.

The Blockchain Sentinel: The Blockchain Security Analyst: Secures blockchain networks and smart contracts, ensuring their integrity.

Now that we've explored the vast sea of cybersecurity careers, you might wonder, "Which path is right for me?" That's a question only you can answer.

Self-Reflection Survey

Consider your interests, strengths, and values to help you uncover the path to your true north.

- What aspects of cybersecurity intrigue you the most?

- Do you prefer hands-on technical work, strategic planning, or a combination of both?

- How do you handle high-pressure situations?

Remember, your journey in cybersecurity is uniquely yours, and the path you choose should reflect your passions and goals. Understanding your strengths, motivations, and aspirations allows you to make informed decisions that align with your true self. It ensures you will choose a path that is both rewarding and sustainable.

CHAPTER FOUR

MAPPING YOUR CYBERSECURITY JOURNEY

"To thine own self be true, and it must follow, as the night the day, thou canst not then be false to any man."

~*William Shakespeare*

Reflecting on my career, I am reminded of the countless crossroads and decisions that have shaped my journey. Each choice, whether deliberate or serendipitous, has contributed to the path I walk today. Many of you may be seeking direction and clarity as you navigate the vast and dynamic field of cybersecurity. Let this chapter be your compass, guiding you toward a more intentional and fulfilling work life.

Throughout my years of mentoring and supporting aspiring tech and cybersecurity professionals—particularly women and minorities—I have observed a recurring theme: their struggle to recognize and embrace their unique strengths and potential.

Too often, I've witnessed diverse students and job candidates allow external expectations and stereotypes to dictate and diminish their professional aspirations. This chapter invites you to take a step back and deeply reevaluate your personal passions, strengths, and areas for growth. Doing so will allow you to hit the reset button and regain control of your career narrative. The goal is to eliminate the external noise and allow your values and ambitions to guide your tech and cybersecurity path.

Remember when I told you about how I struggled with imposter syndrome and fear early in my career, second-guessing every decision and wondering if I belonged in this field? A deep dive into self-reflection and an honest assessment helped me overcome those doubts. And that's what I will help you do for yourself.

The Art of Self-Reflection

It's not always easy to dive deep and self-reflect honestly, especially if you've been conditioned to downplay your achievements or doubt your abilities. Here are some tips to help you get started:

- Be honest with yourself: This isn't about impressing anyone. It's about gaining genuine insights.

- Embrace your unique journey: Your experiences, including the challenges you've faced, have shaped you and are a source of strength.

- Think beyond technical skills. Soft skills like communication, problem-solving, and adaptability are just as crucial in cybersecurity.

- Consider your values: What matters most to you in your career? What kind of impact do you want to make?

- Imagine your future self: Where do you see yourself in the next 5,10 years? What kind of work excites you?

Self-Reflection Survey

With those questions and thoughts in mind, it's time to complete a general self-reflection survey. For each question, I want you to rate yourself on a scale of 1 to 5, where 1 is "Strongly Disagree" and 5 is "Strongly Agree":

____ 1. I am passionate about technology and enjoy keeping up with tech trends.

____ 2. I find satisfaction in solving complex problems.

____ 3. I can explain technical concepts to non-technical people effectively.

____ 4. I work well under pressure and can maintain focus during crises.

____ 5. I enjoy collaborating with others and working in team environments.

____ 6. I am comfortable taking calculated risks.

____ 7. I have a strong ethical compass and prioritize integrity in my work.

___ 8. I am adaptable and can quickly learn new technologies or methodologies.

___ 9. I enjoy taking on leadership roles and guiding others.

___ 10. I am detail-oriented and have a keen eye for spotting inconsistencies.

___ 11. I am curious about how things work and enjoy "tinkering" with systems.

___ 12. I value continuous learning and actively seek out new knowledge.

___ 13. I can see the big picture and think strategically about long-term goals.

___ 14. I am comfortable with ambiguity and don't mind making decisions with incomplete information.

___ 15. I am resilient and can bounce back from setbacks or failures.

Now, I want you to take some time to reflect on your responses. In what areas did you score high, and in which areas did you give yourself a lower score? Do your scores align with your perception of who you are? Were there any surprises?

Cybersecurity Career Compass: A Self-Assessment Tool

Now, let's focus more specifically on cybersecurity career paths. Rate how strongly you agree with each statement on a scale of 1 to 5, where 1 is "Strongly Disagree" and 5 is "Strongly Agree":

___ 1. I enjoy analyzing data and looking for patterns.

___ 2. I like the idea of ethically hacking into systems to find vulnerabilities.

___ 3. I'm fascinated by the technical details of how security systems work.

___ 4. I thrive in high-pressure situations and enjoy solving problems.

___ 5. I enjoy explaining complex concepts and providing strategic advice.

___ 6. I enjoy developing high-level security strategies and policies.

___ 7. I enjoy investigating and piecing together clues to solve puzzles.

___ 8. I'm fascinated by encryption and secure communication methods.

___ 9. I stay up to date with the latest threats and attack methods.

___ 10. I'm interested in securing cloud-based systems and data.

___ 11. I enjoy the intersection of software development and security.

___ 12. I'm excited by emerging technologies like AI and IoT.

___ 13. I enjoy complex projects and bringing together diverse teams.

___ 14. I'm interested in security regulations and managing overall risk.

Interpreting Your Results

- If you scored highest on questions 1 and 9, you might be well-suited for a Security Analyst or Threat Intelligence Analyst role.

- High scores on questions 2 and 3 suggest you might enjoy being a Penetration Tester or Security Engineer.

- If you scored highest on questions 4 and 7, consider exploring roles in Incident Response or Digital Forensics.

- High scores on questions 5 and 6 indicate you might excel as a Security Consultant or CISO.

- If you scored highest on question 8, you might be interested in Cryptography.

- High scores on questions 10 and 11 suggest that Cloud Security or Application Security roles might be a good fit.

- If you scored highest on question 12, you might be well-suited for emerging AI Security or IoT Security roles.

- High scores on question 13 indicate you might excel as a Security Project Manager.

- If you scored highest on question 14, consider exploring roles in Governance, Risk, and Compliance (GRC).

Remember, these results are just a starting point. Use them as a guide to exploring different roles and finding the right path for you.

Cultural Background Reflection

As we dive deeper into self-reflection, it's also crucial for you to consider how your cultural background influences your approach to your cybersecurity career. Being a woman of color in this field has presented unique challenges for me, but I've also gained so many valuable new insights and strengths.

Consider the following questions:

- How has your cultural background influenced your approach to problem-solving?

- Are there aspects of your culture that align well with cybersecurity principles?

- Have you faced any cultural barriers or stereotypes in your cybersecurity journey? How have you navigated these?

- Are there cultural values or practices that you feel could bring unique perspectives to cybersecurity?

- How comfortable do you feel expressing your cultural identity in professional settings?

- Are there role models from your cultural background in cybersecurity that inspire you?

- How has your culture shaped your communication style, and how does this impact your professional interactions?

- Are there any cultural norms regarding career choices or professional behavior you've had to navigate?

Reflecting on these questions can help you recognize the unique strengths and perspectives you bring to the field. It can also help you identify areas where you might need to work on bridging cultural differences in the workplace or challenge existing stereotypes.

Personal SWOT Analysis

Evaluating your Strengths, Weaknesses, Opportunities, and Threats (SWOT) will help you better understand your value, where you have room for improvement, and how to move forward best strategically to advance your cybersecurity career. Grab a notebook and pen, and let's work on your SWOT.

Evaluating Your Strengths

- What technical skills do you excel in?

- What soft skills set you apart?

- What unique perspectives do you bring to cybersecurity?

- What achievements are you most proud of?

- What technical areas do you need to improve?

- Are there soft skills you struggle with?

- Are there aspects of cybersecurity that you find challenging?

- What feedback have you received about areas for improvement?

Evaluating Your Opportunities:

- What emerging trends in cybersecurity align with your interests?

- Are there new roles or technologies you'd like to explore?

- What unique networking or mentorship opportunities can you explore?

- Are there gaps in the industry that your unique background could fill?

- What obstacles might you face in advancing your cybersecurity career?

- Are there industry changes that could impact your chosen path?

- What personal or professional challenges might hinder your progress?

- Are there biases or stereotypes you may need to overcome?

Now that you have completed your SWOT analysis, reflect on the results. How can you leverage your strengths to seize new opportunities? How can you address weaknesses to mitigate your threats?

The goal of doing self-reflection and a personal SWOT early into your career is to help you navigate to the right roles sooner. I've seen many professionals, including me, struggle to transition into a different cybersecurity specialty after realizing they had chosen a path that wasn't the most exciting and challenging. For example, there was a time in my career when I wanted to move from risk management to penetration testing. Despite my enthusiasm and willingness to learn, my manager was reluctant to support me, citing the disruption it would cause the team and the required training investment. This experience taught me a valuable lesson. Getting hired directly into your desired role is often easier than transitioning later. This is not to say it is impossible or impractical to make career transitions from one area of expertise to another. It is your career, and you are the ultimate captain of your destiny.

If you visualize your goals and map the best possible path, the road ahead can be much smoother. If you're starting out or looking to change careers, use the insights gleaned from self-reflection and SWOT analysis to target roles better suited to your aspirations and strengths.

As we wrap up this chapter, I want you to remember that self-reflection is not a one-time exercise. It's a skill and practice that you should revisit regularly throughout your career. Your interests and strengths may shift as you gain new experiences and skills. Embrace and honor your growth, and let it continue to guide your career journey.

Remember, in cybersecurity, your unique perspective is your superpower. The digital world needs your specific set of skills and leadership. Just don't be naive about the tech and cybersecurity industry. Women, especially Black women, may encounter many firewalls.

Personal Reflection

I remember attending my very first major conference as a cybersecurity professional. Walking into the room, I felt excitement and apprehension because there weren't many people in attendance who looked like me. As I began introducing myself to the mostly White male attendees, I sensed subtle, and sometimes not-so-subtle, questioning of my presence and expertise. This is one of many moments that underscored the firewalls I was up against. Incidents like this made me feel I had to prove myself constantly. Over time, I learned to decrypt firewalls like this and many others, including feeling invisible, bouts with imposter syndrome, and colorism.

In the next chapter, I'll help you better understand these challenges and how you can play a vital role in helping to dismantle them to create a more inclusive industry that better reflects the diverse world we live in.

CHAPTER FIVE

DECRYPTING

THE COLORISM FIREWALL

"When we consistently suppress and distrust our intuitive knowingness, looking instead for authority, validation, and approval from others, we give our personal power away."

~*Shakti Gawain*

In the world of cybersecurity, we often talk about firewalls—the digital barriers designed to keep threats at bay. Sadly, in the tech and cybersecurity industry, women, women of color, and African American Black women are often left feeling as if we are the threats.

Modern Day Colorism

Colorism–discrimination based on skin tone–isn't something unique to tech and cybersecurity. It is a broader pervasive issue that still taints the U.S. workplace today. Studies have shown that there is a significant wage gap linked to skin color, with darker-skinned individuals often earning less than their lighter-skinned counterparts. These gaps also show up in other areas, including:

- **Employment:** Colorism affects hiring practices and career advancement. Lighter-skinned individuals are often perceived as more competent. This bias can lead to fewer job prospects and slower career progression for darker-skinned individuals.

- **Representation and Leadership:** When lighter-skinned individuals predominantly occupy leadership roles, it reinforces the notion that lighter skin is associated with competence and authority.

Colorism is not only perpetrated by individuals of different races but also within the same racial or ethnic groups. Interracial discrimination can equally create hostile work environments and affect mental health and job satisfaction.

Scholarly Research

A myriad of published studies underscore the psychological, emotional, and socioeconomic impacts of colorism on communities of color. One such study is a *Frontiers in Sociology* article that explores the relationship between colorism and immigrant earnings in the United States. The study found that immigrants with darker skin color face a substantial earnings penalty, highlighting the ongoing issue of colorism in the labor market. Another study published in the *Journal of Colorism Studies* also highlights the psychological, emotional, and socioeconomic impacts of colorism on communities of color.

The ugly fact remains that colorism continues to be a significant barrier to equality and inclusion in the workplace. Addressing this issue will require a concerted effort from organizations to implement regular unconscious bias training for employees. Organizations must also continue to advocate for and promote diversity and inclusion initiatives to ensure the fair representation of individuals with diverse skin tones in leadership positions.

My Color Firewall

If you are like me, a woman with a darker complexion, you've likely encountered experiences in your lifetime that have made you feel like your skin color was a firewall. I can honestly say there have been moments in my life where I wished I had the power to be invisible.

The memories that trouble me the most are those from my early childhood. I can remember, just like it was yesterday, a traumatic experience I endured on Easter Sunday when I was just five years old. That morning, I couldn't wait to get up and wear the new pastel dress my mother had picked out just for me. As we arrived at church, I felt a sense of pride and excitement wearing it. I looked forward to seeing everyone else all dressed up, too. But as I walked along with my lighter-skinned cousins to greet other church members, none of them ever acknowledged me or my new dress. Instead, they only complimented my fair-skinned cousins, which was hurtful and confusing. It was the first time I felt different. But even at five years old, it is evident in my blossoming little mind that my much darker skin was the blaring difference. At that moment, I felt invisible. This experience with colorism was my first, but it was far from my last. It was significant because this moment in my early childhood planted a seed of doubt that grew over the years. A persistent internal voice, always whispering that I wasn't pretty enough or good enough. I was a brown-skinned girl with short, kinky, steel wool hair, ashy knees, big brown eyes, and skinny bird legs. I was born imperfect, according to the subculture in my backyard that defined me, and because of that, I didn't feel important or seen.

Nobody in my family ever called me ugly, but none of them ever called me pretty. I often heard other girls being complimented about their hair and skin color when I was standing just inches away, and not so much as a word was uttered about me, which made me insecure. And even though I've always been told by my parents and loved ones not to listen to what others say, I can't deny that words hurt. The old saying, "Sticks and stones may break my bones, but words will never hurt me," is a lie. Words do hurt. Words matter. And I began to lean on the words of others and give them more merit than my own. They eventually poisoned my spirit. I lost my self-esteem, and as I grew older, I lost my voice.

My personal story is a testament that the ideologies of colorism can have a crippling impact. Learning at such a young age that dark brown girls are treated differently and not in a good way because of their complexion and the texture of their hair was too much for my young mind to comprehend.

It took me decades to learn to release my past. Through positive affirmations and self-talk, I learned to rebuild my confidence. Like a reflection in a mirror, I stopped looking at myself through the eyes of others. I used to say I would feel better about myself "if." For so long, I allowed the word "if" to control my life and hold me back. When I began showing myself compassion and stopped comparing myself to others, I no longer felt like an average B-Girl. I decided I could be an "A, B, C, D, E, or F" girl—Awesome, Brave, Courageous, Dynamic, Extraordinary, and Fabulous.

I share my painful story because, as women of color, we often carry the trauma associated with the way the world sees us from childhood into adulthood. You can and should release this burden because you are indeed *"Magic,"* and don't you ever forget it. Women of color need to recognize that we are not alone. In a world where the spotlight is often on gender, race, and disability bias, colorism is frequently overlooked. But it is equally harmful. A silent sorting algorithm in our workplace must be addressed to create a more inclusive and equitable workforce.

But here's the good news. Just like with any algorithm, once you understand it, you can work to change it. In cybersecurity, we're trained to identify vulnerabilities and patch them. It's time we applied that same rigor to these societal and corporate vulnerabilities.

Understanding and Overcoming Imposter Syndrome

They say the devil is in the details, and it's true. Another ugly detail that you will likely grapple with as a woman and person of color is Imposter Syndrome: that nagging feeling that you're a fraud despite clear evidence of your competence and achievements. Imposter Syndrome is the little voice in your head that says, "I don't really belong here," "I'm not ready," or "I just got lucky." It's a psychological phenomenon that can affect anyone, regardless of gender, age, or level of success.

Yes, you read that right—even though many women and people of color talk about experiencing Imposter Syndrome, anyone can experience it, even men who exude major confidence. Imposter Syndrome is serious because when you constantly second-guess yourself, you're less likely to take reasonable risks, share innovative ideas, or apply for leadership roles for which you're qualified. In a field as dynamic and critical as cybersecurity, we can't afford to let self-doubt hold us back.

Recognizing you may have Imposter Syndrome and addressing it early on could be the key to unlocking your full potential. So, how do you know if you may be experiencing imposter syndrome? Here are some self-reflection questions that can help:

- Do you often attribute your success to luck or external factors rather than your own abilities?

- Do you find it difficult to accept compliments about your work?

- Are you afraid of being considered incompetent in your role by others?

- Do you downplay your expertise, even in areas where you are genuinely knowledgeable?

- Do you feel you need to perform everything perfectly, or else you've failed?

If you answered "yes" to three or more of these questions, you might be experiencing Imposter Syndrome. But remember, recognizing it is the first step towards overcoming it.

Coping with the Imposter Within

As I've grappled with Imposter Syndrome over the years, I've discovered some strategies that have helped me confront my feelings head-on. I'm sharing these strategies to help you relinquish any doubt that the tech and cybersecurity industry needs your gifts. As Dr. Valerie Young, an expert on Imposter Syndrome, notes, "Naming the fear can knock the wind out of it."

When I started opening up to trusted colleagues and mentors about my feelings, I was surprised to learn how many had experienced the same struggles. Our shared vulnerability created stronger bonds between us and helped me realize I wasn't alone. Another crucial step was learning to rewire my system to think differently and assess my abilities realistically. I started keeping a "Success Journal" where I documented my accomplishments, no matter how small. I incorporated positive self-talk and stopped saying I couldn't, but "Yes, I can."

On days when my internal imposter voice was particularly loud, I flipped through my Success Journal, reminding myself of the concrete evidence of my competence. This practice helped me challenge my irrational beliefs about myself.

I also learned to stop constantly comparing myself to others. In our field of cybersecurity, it's easy to feel like everyone else is more knowledgeable and capable. However, I realized I fueled my feelings of inadequacy whenever I compared myself to others. Instead, I began focusing on my unique strengths and contributions.

Diversity of thought and experience is what makes our field strong. Your unique perspective is valuable, even if (especially if) it's different from others. One of my most powerful shifts was learning to reframe my imposter feelings as a sign of growth. If you're feeling like an imposter, it often means you're pushing yourself out of your comfort zone. You're taking on new challenges and expanding your skills. Instead of seeing these feelings as a sign of fraudulence, I've learned to see them as indicators that I'm growing and evolving in my career.

Lastly, perhaps most importantly, I've learned not to let these feelings hold me back. Even when the imposter's voice is whispering doubts, I push forward. I took on that challenging project, spoke up in that meeting, and applied for that promotion. As I practice these behaviors, they have become a part of who I am; they're etched into my DNA. Because here's the truth: You don't have to feel 100% confident to be competent. Action often comes before confidence, not the other way around. If you're struggling with imposter syndrome, I encourage you to try these nine strategies:

1. Share your feelings with a trusted friend or mentor.

2. Keep a record of your accomplishments and review them regularly.

3. Focus on your unique strengths rather than comparing yourself to others.

4. Reframe imposter feelings as signs of growth and challenge.

5. Take action despite your fears.

6. Support others as a way to alleviate feelings of inadequacy. By serving others, you can discover your true value and capabilities.

7. Surround yourself with positive people. We are the sum of the five people in our closet circle. It might be time to audit your circle.

8. Seek constructive feedback from trusted colleagues, mentors, or supervisors. Their insights can provide valuable perspectives and help you see your strengths more clearly.

9. Take time to celebrate your accomplishments with people who are genuinely happy for you, no matter how small they may seem.

Remember, overcoming Imposter Syndrome is a journey, not a destination. There will be days when insecure feelings creep in, but with practice, you'll better recognize and challenge them. If Imposter Syndrome significantly impacts your life or career, don't hesitate to seek professional help. A mental health professional can provide additional strategies and support tailored to your situation.

Unpacking Microaggressions

As I navigate my career in cybersecurity, I've found that microaggressions can also profoundly impact women's careers, especially those of us with marginalized identities. Even high-profile Tech executive and philanthropist Sheryl Sandberg has spoken out about experiencing microaggressions.

Imagine you're in a meeting, presenting a groundbreaking idea for a new security protocol. Suddenly, a male colleague interrupts you mid-sentence and talks over you as if you weren't even there.

~Sheryl Sandberg

Sandberg had barely started her career when she noticed how often she was interrupted mid-sentence. "Even to this day, when I am in meetings with the same seniority as the other people, I still get interrupted more than men," she shared while speaking at a conference. If Sandberg, one of the world's most recognized business executives, is still being spoken over in meetings, can you imagine what it is like for women in the workplace worldwide? According to LeanIn.org's latest *Women in the Workplace* report with McKinsey & Co., women are more than twice as likely as men to be interrupted when presenting. This statistic highlights a pervasive issue that affects women across all levels regardless of their professional hierarchy. Microaggressions like these not only undermine women's contributions but also perpetuate a culture where their voices are marginalized.

Addressing this issue is crucial to fostering a more inclusive and equitable workplace culture where everyone thrives. For women of color, the situation is even more challenging. The same study revealed that Asian and Black women are 7x more likely than women overall to be confused with someone of the same race and ethnicity. As a Black woman in tech, I've experienced this firsthand, and let me tell you, it's not just embarrassing; it's demoralizing. But what exactly are microaggressions? The term was first coined in the 1970s by Harvard psychiatrist Chester Pierce and later expanded upon by Columbia University psychologist Derald Wing Sue.

Sue defines microaggressions as the everyday slights, indignities, put-downs, and insults that members of marginalized groups experience in their day-to-day interactions with individuals who are often unaware that they have engaged in an offensive or demeaning way. LeanIn.org study found that women who experience microaggressions are over three times more likely to struggle with burnout or consider quitting their jobs. For women from marginalized groups, the numbers are even more stark.

Dealing with microaggressions can be challenging, but there are several strategies you can use to address and counter them effectively:

- **Acknowledge and Validate:** Recognize that microaggressions are real and validate your feelings. It's important to acknowledge the impact they have on you and others.

- **Respond in the Moment:** If you feel comfortable, address microaggression immediately. You can use phrases like "I don't think that's appropriate" or "Can you explain what you mean by that?" This can help raise awareness of the issue without escalating the situation[1].

- **Seek Support:** Talk to trusted colleagues, mentors, or friends about your experiences. They can offer support and advice and sometimes even intervene on your behalf.

- **Document Incidents:** Record microaggressions, including dates, times, and descriptions of what happened. This can be useful if you report the behavior to HR or a supervisor.

- **Educate and Advocate:** Use these moments to educate others about microaggressions and their impact. Advocate for training and policies that promote a more inclusive and respectful workplace[2].

- **Practice Self-Care:** Engage in activities that help you manage stress and maintain your well-being. This could include exercise, meditation, or spending time with supportive people.

- **Bystander Intervention:** If you witness a microaggression, speak up. Simple statements like, "That's not okay," or "I don't agree with that," can help support the person targeted and discourage the behavior[5].

- **Reflect and Decide:** Consider the context and your relationship with the person who committed the microaggression. Decide whether it's worth addressing immediately, later, or letting it go. Sometimes, choosing your battles is a strategic way to manage your energy and well-being[1].

- **Formal Reporting:** If microaggressions persist, report them to HR or use formal organizational complaint mechanisms. Having documented incidents can strengthen your case.

- **Training and Workshops:** Encourage your organization to provide diversity, equity, and inclusion training. These programs can help raise awareness and reduce the occurrence of microaggressions[2].

Using these strategies, you can create a more inclusive environment and help mitigate the impact of microaggressions in the workplace. For those in leadership positions, it's crucial to create a culture where microaggressions are not tolerated. For example, if you see a woman on your team being interrupted during a meeting, interject and allow her an opportunity to finish sharing her insights. This also means implementing microaggression training programs, establishing clear reporting mechanisms to address them, and holding people accountable for their behavior toward others.

Navigating Multiple Identities

Perhaps one of the most courageous acts is carrying the banner for both your gender and your race. It's like running two firewalls simultaneously, each requiring constant vigilance and energy to maintain the other.

Below are some personal strategies that have helped me and can help you navigate the cybersecurity maze:

- **Build Your Network Firewall:** Seek out and connect with other women in cybersecurity to receive support and mentorship and to access a safe space to share experiences and strategies.

- **Upgrade Your Confidence Software:** Document your achievements. Keep a "brag file" of your successes, big and small. When imposter syndrome strikes, review this file to remind yourself of your capabilities.

- **Implement a Strong Authentication System:** Don't let others define your worth. Develop a strong sense of self and stand firm in your knowledge and abilities.

- **Run Regular Security Audits:** Continuously assess your skills and identify areas for growth. The tech world moves fast, and staying current is crucial for confidence and career advancement.

- **Encrypt Your Communication:** Learn to communicate assertively without falling into the "aggressive" trap. Practice clear, confident communication that leaves no room for misinterpretation.

- **Deploy Visibility Protocols:** Make your contributions known. Speak up in meetings, volunteer for high-visibility projects, and ensure your name is associated with your work.

- **Activate Your Allies:** Identify and cultivate relationships with allies who can amplify your voice and advocate for you when you're not in the room.

- **Install a Self-Care Firewall:** Dealing with these challenges can be emotionally draining. Prioritize self-care and mental health to prevent burnout.

As I look back on my journey from the hood to the C-suite, I realize that each challenge I faced was a line of code in my personal growth algorithm.

Every setback, every microaggression, and every moment of self-doubt made me the resilient, successful cybersecurity professional I am today. But my story isn't unique. It's a narrative shared by many women, especially women of color, in this field.

Remember, in the world of cybersecurity, diversity isn't just a "nice-to-have"; it's a critical defense against "groupthink" and homogeneous problem-solving. Your unique perspective, shaped by your experiences as a woman, a person of color, and whoever you are, is invaluable. So, the next time you feel invisible, remember you're not a ghost in the machine. You're an essential part of the system, a critical line of code in the program of progress. It's time we help decrypt the double firewall for future generations. In the end, true cybersecurity isn't just about protecting systems and data. It's about creating a diverse, inclusive industry where everyone's talents shine. That's a firewall worth building.

CHAPTER SIX

NAVIGATING MENTORSHIP, AUTHENTICITY & NETWORKING

"Success is no accident. It is hard work, perseverance, learning, studying, sacrifice and most of all, it's loving what you are doing or learning to do."

~*Pele*

The world of cybersecurity is vast and ever-changing, like a digital ocean with currents of data flowing in every direction. And just like the sea, it offers countless paths for exploration and adventure. Reflecting on my career, from the Navy to the civilian tech world, I realize how crucial mentorship, authenticity, and networking have been in shaping my path.

As a Black woman in cybersecurity, I've often felt like I was navigating uncharted territories without a map or compass. The lack of mentors who looked like me or shared my experiences made the journey far more challenging than it needed to be. I remember the early days of my career, fresh out of the Navy and eager to make my mark in the civilian tech world. I was brimming with enthusiasm, armed with technical skills and a drive to succeed. But I quickly realized that technical prowess alone wasn't enough to navigate the complex currents of the corporate world.

While I continued to race for the corporate boardroom, I did not actually get there until I created my own stage. As a young adult out of the Navy, I had a vision for myself—excelling in life and having a seat in the executive boardroom. The challenge was that no one could give me a career map of how to get there, and no one warned me that the path was not a straight climb up the ladder. No one prepared me for the broken ladder I

would encounter. I wasn't told there may be steps missing from the ladder. Nor was I taught the strategies to climb over the missing rungs in the ladder.

But every obstacle I faced has given me pearls of wisdom to share with the next generation of tech and cybersecurity leaders. Through it all, I have become a positive force for change within myself and the world.

I got my first technology job as a radioman technical controller while serving in the United States Navy. My work entailed troubleshooting and maintaining telecommunications systems, changing out encryption keys, and learning the call path network flow. My military job helped me learn the importance of teamwork and networking. The military taught me the soft skills that later made me successful as a leader.

When I met with the recruiter preparing to enlist in the military, my father told me, "Cheryl, make sure you select a job category that will provide you with excellent transferable skills." My father was an Army War Veteran who was well trained in how to survive in battle, but he was honest in sharing that when he got out of the military, he had no transferable skills for civilian work. I knew the power of technology and how the next generation of technology would change the world.

I worked hard and was promoted several times throughout my military career, boosting my confidence and belief in my capabilities. I served honorably for eight years before pursuing career opportunities outside of the military. I was ready to learn and contribute to advancing technology and cybersecurity.

Upon leaving the Navy, I had a stellar resume, having received a great deal of training and many accolades for my community work while serving as a color guard in the Navy. I found my first civilian job after leaving the military at Teleconnect, a telecommunications company in Cedar Rapids, Iowa. There, I continued to perfect my trade, learning more about troubleshooting, fixing, and repairing technology.

I quickly grew and advanced my skills, but just as I was in talks to be promoted to supervisor of the Teleconnect Operations Control Center, my mother had a stroke. With my mom's health failing, I decided to leave my position so that I could move closer to her home in Kansas City to help care for her. I also used this time to reset and really map out where I wanted to go next. I was ready to give Corporate America my best shot and began seeking opportunities at a Fortune 100 Internet service provider company in the Kansas City area. Soon, I landed a job as a Network Operations Control specialist at this very company. My role involved troubleshooting and analyzing performance issues within the network, which allowed me to present the "Big C" customer presentations. It helped me become a stronger presenter and garnered more visibility from higher-ups in the company.

My voice was getting stronger, and I was building my personal brand, so to speak. It was always vital for me to have goals and a game plan. I was always refining how to develop myself and bring the most value to the organizations I served. This included being ready and eager to take on new opportunities. For example, there was an instance when my boss walked into the Control Center and asked if anyone would like to drive to Omaha, Nebraska, to shadow field technicians to see how they spliced broken fibers. I quickly raised my hand, grabbed some snacks and my coat, and hopped on the highway headed to Nebraska.

That same night, I was out on a live railroad site. It was dark, with no streetlights or sidewalks, just railroad tracks as far as the eye could see. It was freezing that night, around 34 degrees. The technicians had a tent with all the splicing equipment and a campfire to help keep us warm. We drank coffee, hot chocolate, and even roasted hot dogs. If you had to go to the bathroom, you either used the port-a-potty or grabbed a roll and went deep into the woods. It was bare-bones living while working.

The crew I shadowed had to complete their assignment by 7:00 a.m. the next day when the maintenance window would close. They allowed me to do some fiber splicing, and I have to admit, it was pretty hilarious. I learned that night that their job wasn't easy. Imagine trying to take two pieces of sewing thread and match them up perfectly end-to-end, where you cannot see or feel the break in the thread. That's what it was like repairing and splicing fiber. It took me more than three times to get a single splice done, but finally, I could connect two fibers. The following day, we all gathered our things to head our separate ways, but not before I thanked the guys for letting me observe and giving me some hands-on training. I thought I would never see any of those geniuses again.

Several guys from that same Omaha Control Center came to Kansas City some years later. They invited me out for drinks, and before I knew it, I had been building a new network of colleagues who had become life-long friends and supporters over the years.

I learned many valuable lessons from this crew, including new ways of thinking and approaching my work. However, even as I grew more experienced and skilled, I still had no promotion opportunities in the company. I was applying for more senior roles, but time and time again, I was told that I either needed more experience or wasn't a good fit.

This didn't sit right with me for several reasons, but mainly because, in many cases, I was already doing the work required for the role I was applying for. Often, the people they hired had less experience and needed to be trained by me. Needless to say, it was devastating. I had purchased the designer suits and high-heeled shoes that I saw other leaders wearing. I styled my hair straight and wore it back in a tight professional bun. I had earned all my colleagues' degrees and special certifications, but still, I couldn't land a promotion.

Back then, the prevailing belief and sentiment from others was that I should be grateful, even on cloud nine, because I was employed, drove a Cadillac, owned a lovely home, and could keep food on the table. However, to the contrary, I was not happy. There were so many unwritten rules, subtle dynamics, and invisible barriers that I had to learn to navigate independently. So, my advice to anyone is to find your voice early. I wasn't confident enough back then to call out what I knew was happening in a way that could help me overcome it. Instead, I bottled up my feelings. Often wondering:

- What if they don't like what I say?

- What if they laugh at what I say?

- What if what I say doesn't make sense?

But mostly, I was afraid to speak up because I didn't want to earn the dreaded title of "The Angry Black Woman," a stereotype that portrays the Black woman as ill-tempered, ignorant, and hostile. So, I stayed silent and allowed my work to do the talking, which eventually paid off.

After leading Network Operations, Disaster Recovery and Business Continuity, and Training organizations for a company with 70,000 employees, I became a project manager in the IT Department. You must have allies in corporate America, so I seized this opportunity to grow my network and build new relationships. I also began doing more personal research to understand better why it was so hard for Black leaders to progress in Corporate America. The statistics are stunning.

According to a 2019 CBS News Report, Black professionals hold only 3.2% of executive jobs and 0.8% of all Fortune 500 CEO positions. The numbers for Latinos and Asians are comparable. Associate Professor of Business Laura Morgan Roberts suggested in a Harvard Business Review article that stats like these could mean companies and senior leadership either "unconsciously or consciously don't offer equal access to opportunity growth based on their own biases."

This is why sponsorship is so important and impactful. The influence of sponsors can help a qualified candidate with a diverse background unlock doors to bigger roles and responsibilities within an organization. As the COO of Facebook, Sheryl Sandberg, aptly put it, "Mentorship and sponsorship are key drivers of success." And national HR and DEI leader Karen Wilkens-Mickey said senior leaders serving as sponsors "should be embedded in the fabric of a company's culture."

These experts mean that sponsorship and mentorship are not just about providing guidance; it's about creating a support system that empowers individuals to reach their full potential. It's sharing knowledge, offering encouragement, stepping into the ring, and putting your name on the line to help others you know deserve it advance and better navigate the complexities of their careers. We can break down barriers and create a more inclusive and diverse workforce through sponsorship and mentorship.

Effective Mentorship: Paying It Forward

As you progress in your career, you'll likely find opportunities to become a mentor yourself. This can be an incredibly rewarding experience, allowing you to give back to your community and help shape the future of our field. Here are some tips for being an effective mentor:

1. Listen Actively: Sometimes, your mentee needs someone to listen to their concerns and validate their experiences. As Stephen R. Covey wisely said, "Most people do not listen with the intent to understand; they listen with the intent to reply." Break this pattern and truly listen.

2. Share Your Experiences: Don't be afraid to discuss your failures and successes. Your mentee can learn valuable lessons from both.

3. Provide Honest Feedback: Constructive criticism, delivered with kindness, can be one of the most valuable gifts you can give your mentee.

4. Celebrate Their Successes: Be your mentee's biggest cheerleader. Recognize and celebrate their achievements, no matter how small.

5. Connect Them with Others: Use your network to open doors for your mentee when appropriate.

6. Encourage Independence: The goal is to empower your mentee, not to make them dependent on you. Encourage them to think critically and make their own decisions.

Remember, mentorship is a two-way street. You'll likely learn just as much from your mentees as they learn from you.

The Role of Allies in Career Development

While mentors and sponsors are crucial in career development, allies are equally important. Allies use their privilege or position to advocate for and support underrepresented groups.

In my career, allies have been instrumental in opening doors, amplifying my voice, and creating growth opportunities. I recall a pivotal moment early in my career when a senior executive, a white male, took notice of my work. He praised my contributions in team meetings and recommended me for high-visibility projects. His allyship gave me the exposure and opportunities to advance my career. More and more highly visible leaders like Melinda Gates are giving voice to the power of Allyship.

"Allyship is about taking action to champion people from underrepresented groups, and it's one of the most effective ways we can fight inequality."

~Melinda Gates

If you're in a position of privilege, consider how you can serve as an ally to underrepresented individuals in your organization.

Building Your Cybersecurity Community

In the rapidly evolving world of cybersecurity, your network can be your best asset. Building a strong professional network isn't just about collecting business cards or adding connections on LinkedIn. You need to work on building a community of peers, mentors, and allies who can support you throughout your career. Here are some strategies for networking with purpose:

- **Define Your Goals:** Before you start networking, take some time to think about what you want to achieve. Having clear goals will help you focus your networking efforts and make meaningful connections.

- **Attend Industry Events:** Conferences, workshops, and seminars are excellent opportunities to meet professionals in your field. Participate actively by asking questions and engaging in discussions.

- **Leverage Online Platforms:** Use platforms like LinkedIn to build your professional network. Engage with your connections' posts, share interesting articles, and don't be afraid to reach out for virtual coffee chats.

- **Join Professional Organizations:** Organizations like WiCyS, ISACA, ISC², and ISSA offer numerous networking opportunities. Get involved in local chapters and participate in online forums.

- **Create Value for Others**: Networking isn't just about what others can do for you; it's also about what you can offer. Share your knowledge and experiences and be a supportive colleague.

- **Follow-Up and Nurture Relationships:** Building strong professional relationships takes time and effort. Follow up with new connections and keep in touch regularly.

- **Be Authentic**: Don't try to be someone you're not. Authenticity is key to building meaningful, lasting professional relationships.

The Power of Being You

Renowned researcher and author Brene Brown defines authenticity as "The daily practice of letting go of who we think we're supposed to be and embracing who we are." I tried to fit into a box for much of my professional life. I spoke and dressed as others thought I should. As a Black woman, I did everything I could to distract from the color of my skin. I tried to fit into a mold, to conform to what I thought was expected of me. I spoke and dressed in a way that felt inauthentic, trying to downplay my Blackness in a white space. I believed that conforming was the key to success. But here's the thing: It left me feeling empty, disconnected from my true self.

It wasn't until later in life that I realized the power of authenticity. This meant acknowledging and celebrating my identity as a Black woman, with all the unique experiences and perspectives that come with it. Embracing authenticity has been transformative for me. I am reaching heights I never dreamed possible by staying true to who I am. I have found a sense of freedom and confidence that has allowed me to excel in my career and personal life. There is power in knowing that no one else can replicate my story, experiences, and uniqueness.

Personal Growth & Industry Impact

Reflecting on my journey, I'm reminded of a pivotal experience that crystallized the importance of authenticity and representation in our field. Observing the lack of women, I created a recruitment program proposal targeting underserved female students and submitted it to my executive leadership team. To my delight, they enthusiastically agreed, and I was tapped to help champion the initiative.

In 2022, I led a company first: An "All-Girls Cybersecurity and Technology Career Festival, welcoming 265 diverse female students. It was beyond extraordinary. That experience led me to build a new Cybersecurity Paid Internship Program that I plan to launch for high school juniors and seniors. The program will help students explore potential career opportunities and provide certification while studying in college. Imagine a future where, at the age of 20, students entering the tech and cybersecurity workforce already have certifications, a degree, and four years of experience. That's the kind of transformation we can collectively bring about in the industry.

Paying it Forward: Tips for Being an Effective Mentee

With everything you learn in life, you must be willing to pay forward. That is what makes being a mentor or a sponsor so phenomenal. It's a two-way street. Here are some tried and true tips for mentors and mentees:

1. **Be Proactive:** Don't wait for your mentor to always initiate contact. Reach out regularly, schedule meetings, and come prepared with topics you want to discuss.

2. **Set Clear Goals:** Set clear goals so that both you and your mentor know how to focus your efforts.

3. **Give Advice and Ideas:** Share your wisdom and tangible ideas that can help your mentee navigate any setbacks and thrive.

4. **Show Appreciation:** Recognize that your mentor is investing their time and energy in your growth. Express your gratitude regularly.

5. **Follow Through:** If your mentor gives you advice or suggests a course of action, try to follow through. Report back on your progress or challenges.

6. **Be Respectful of Time:** Your mentor has many commitments. Be punctual in meetings and use the time wisely.

7. **Share Your Successes:** Let your mentor know when you've achieved a goal or milestone. They'll appreciate knowing their guidance has made a difference.

8. **Pay It Forward:** As you grow in your career, look for opportunities to mentor others. This is how we create a cycle of support and growth in our industry.

As management expert Peter Drucker said, "The best way to predict the future is to create it." By being an active and engaged mentee, you're taking a crucial step in creating your future in cybersecurity.

Your Role in Shaping the Future of Cybersecurity

As we wrap up this chapter, I want to leave you with a challenge to create the best supportive tech and cybersecurity community possible. Whether you're just starting your cybersecurity journey or a seasoned professional, having a strong and powerful network is essential for personal and professional growth.

Here are some strategies to help you build and nurture such a community:

Join Professional Organizations

Consider groups such as Women in CyberSecurity (WiCyS) as well as local cybersecurity meetup groups that offer networking opportunities, resources, and support.

Engage in Networking

- Participate in cybersecurity conferences, workshops, and seminars. These events are great for meeting like-minded professionals and expanding your network.

- Join online forums, LinkedIn groups, and social media communities focused on cybersecurity. Engaging in discussions and sharing knowledge can help you connect with others in the field.

Promote Inclusivity and Diversity

- Support initiatives that promote diversity and inclusion within the cybersecurity community. This can include participating in panels, writing articles, or organizing events highlighting the importance of a diverse workforce.

- Foster environments where everyone feels welcome and valued. Encourage open dialogue and respect for different perspectives.

Collaborate on Projects

- Seek out collaborative cybersecurity projects with peers. Partnering can lead to new innovative solutions and strengthen professional relationships.

- Participate in hackathons and cybersecurity competitions. These events provide opportunities to learn, collaborate, and showcase your skills.

Share Knowledge and Resources

- Organize and attend workshops and webinars to share knowledge and learn from others. These events can cover a wide range of topics, from technical skills to career development.

- Create and share resources such as articles, tutorials, and tools that can help others in the community.

Support Each Other

- Acknowledge and celebrate the achievements of your peers. Positive reinforcement can boost morale and foster a supportive atmosphere.

- Be willing to offer assistance and support to others. Whether providing feedback on a project or offering career advice, small acts of kindness can make a big difference.

Stay Connected

- Maintain regular contact with your network. This can be through scheduled meetings, casual catch-ups, or online interactions.

- After meeting someone new, follow up with a message or email to keep the connection alive.

- Building such a community takes time and effort, but the rewards are worth it. When we bring diverse perspectives to the table, we're better equipped to tackle cybersecurity's complex, ever-evolving challenges.

As we wrap up our discussion on the importance of mentorship, authenticity, and networking in cybersecurity, it's time to turn our attention to the technical skills that form the backbone of this field.

CHAPTER SEVEN

WOMEN'S POWER MOVES IN MALE-DOMINATED INDUSTRIES

*"Education is the most powerful weapon
which you can use to change the world."*

~ *Nelson Mandela*

This chapter focuses on "Power Move," strategies that can help you thrive as a woman in male-dominated industries. I've compiled real stories that offer practical strategies that you can begin implementing right away, especially if you've ever:

- Had your voice drowned out in meetings

- Watched less qualified colleagues get promoted over you

- Been excluded from important discussions or decisions

- Found yourself being the "only one" in the room

- Had to work twice as hard to get half the recognition or, even worse, no recognition at all

You'll learn why these things happen and what you can do to stay motivated, on track, and keep moving forward in pursuit of your dreams.

Strategy 1: Commanding the Room

Let me tell you about my mentee, Marge, a brilliant software architect. Marge is the only woman on a team of twelve developers. Despite having the most experience, she constantly found herself being talked over or ignored during technical discussions.

One day, she was ready to quit after a particularly frustrating meeting where her security recommendation was dismissed (only to be enthusiastically received when proposed by a male colleague later). Instead, she gathered herself and reached out to me. Together, we decided quitting was not the path she wanted to take. Instead, after a long talk, we worked to develop her new "Presence Protocol." I got the idea from an article written by Sheryl Sandberg in 2013 entitled, *Lean In: Women, Work and the Will to Lead.*

The Presence Protocol is a comprehensive strategy for making your presence and contributions impossible to ignore in professional settings. It goes beyond just speaking up.

It's a systematic approach to ensuring your voice is heard, your ideas are acknowledged, and your expertise is recognized. What makes it effective is the combination of three crucial elements:

- Physical & Strategic Presence Strategies (how you occupy space and position your contributions)

- Vocal Presence Strategies (how you communicate)

- Follow-Up Strategies (intentional follow-up and follow-through)

Physical & Strategic Presence Strategies

- **Strategic Seating:** Choose central, visible positions in meetings

- **Body Language Optimization:** Open posture, direct eye contact

- **Purposeful Movement:** Controlled, deliberate gestures

- **Space Utilization:** Taking up appropriate physical space at the table

- **Arrive Timely:** Being early to claim space and set up effectively

- **Strategic Positioning:** Arriving early to meetings to choose a seat at the center of the table, not the edges.

Vocal Presence Strategies

- The "Broken Record" Technique: When interrupted, calmly say, "I'd like to finish my point," and continue speaking. No apologies, no room for debate.

- Amplification Approach: Build alliances with other team members ahead of time who agree and will reinforce your points, which makes your contributions harder to ignore.

- Contribute early and meaningfully
  - Use clear, assertive language
  - Document key points and decisions
  - Handle interruptions professionally
  - Support and amplify allies

Follow Up Strategies

- Send follow-up summaries
- Document decisions and contributions
- Schedule relevant follow-up meetings
- Track action items and progress
- Maintain visibility through updates

Marge began implementing a combination of each of these strategies during her regular team meetings. It took some time, but just at the three-month mark, she has moved from wanting to quit to leading technical discussions and loving her job. When a few male colleagues shared how proud they were of her hard work, Marge told them how she was feeling and how she had been working on ways to get her ideas heard. To her surprise, they admitted not knowing they were dismissing her input. Just think, not only did Marge turn things around and begin to enjoy her role, but she also helped her male teammates uncover behavior they were doing unconsciously and not intentionally. Awareness is a big step towards systemic change.

Navigating the Promotion Paradox

Being promoted is a highlight of anyone's career. A tangible and significant reward that lets you know your hard work and dedication is paying off. But there are times in almost everyone's career when they apply for a promotion or a more senior role and aren't hired. It can be a crushing blow to your confidence. But it hurts even worse when you learn that a less qualified person got the role. I experienced this firsthand early in my career, and it taught me some valuable lessons. I was passed over for a senior management position despite having better metrics, more experience, and stronger team relationships than the person who got the role. I'd assumed my work would speak for itself, a rookie error. Afterward, instead of sulking, I devised a strategy to showcase my work better in the future. It has served me well and helped numerous women I've mentored. Here are the steps:

Create A Visibility Portfolio

- Keep a detailed record of your achievements
- Quantify your impacts wherever possible
- Collect testimonials from clients and colleagues
- Document any additional responsibilities you've taken on

Adopt A Strategic Self-Promotion Plan

- Schedule regular updates with decision-makers
- Share wins in public forums
- Create visibility for your team's successes

- Build relationships across departments

Take A Parallel Path

- Don't wait for recognition—create opportunities
- Start leading before you have the title
- Build your external professional profile
- Develop unique expertise that makes you indispensable

There are also strategic ways you can begin to lead without a title by focusing on creating value and building influence. Here's some immediate action steps you can take:

- Identify a gap in your organization that you can fill
- Take the lead on a small initiative that has a measurable impact
- Build a support network of peers who can amplify your efforts
- Document your contributions and impact
- Share your knowledge and expertise generously
- Ask your manager for more complex and challenging projects to show off your skills. Don't wait.
- Look for leadership opportunities to volunteer outside the workplace with not-for-profit organizations.

Remember, leadership is about influence, not position.

Building Unshakeable Confidence

Now, let's address something deeper: Confidence. Not the surface-level "fake it till you make it" kind, but real, unshakeable confidence that stays with you even when you're the only woman in a room of 50 men.

I remember feeling like an impostor despite years of experience several times throughout my career. The turning point came when I realized something crucial. Confidence isn't about never doubting yourself; it's about moving forward despite those doubts. It's like courage; we move forward despite our doubts and fears. I learned some really cool strategies for peak performance and building confidence at a Tony Robbins conference. Here are some of the key takeaways I jotted down while there:

Identifying and Dismantling Limiting Beliefs

"I need to wait to be recognized."

-Replace with: "I create my own opportunities for recognition."

Daily Practice: Document an achievement each day

Action Step: Share one accomplishment in each team meeting

"I'm being too aggressive if I speak up."

-Replace with: "I am confidently contributing valuable insights."

Daily Practice: Do power poses for two minutes before meetings

Action Step: Contribute one strong opinion in every discussion.

"I don't belong in this industry."

-Replace with: "My unique perspective adds essential value."

Daily Practice: Journal about one unique contribution you made

Action Step: Share an insight only your perspective could bring

"I'm not technical/qualified enough"

-Replace with: "I'm constantly growing, and I am valuable."

Daily Practice: Learn one new industry fact or skill daily

Action Step: Regular learning sessions and share knowledge

Energy Management Tips for Peak Work Performance

Morning Peak Routines to help kick-start your workdays:

1. Physical Priming (15 minutes)

- 5 Minutes of Power Poses
- 5 Minutes of High-Energy Aerobic Activity 5 Minutes of Deep Breathing

2. Mental Priming (15 minutes)

- Review Your Achievement Wall (If you don't have one, create one)
- Read Your Personal Power Statements
- Visualize Successful Meeting Interactions

3. Strategic Priming (15 minutes)

- Review daily objectives
- Envision How Meetings Will Go
- Energy Management Throughout the Day

4. Pre-Meeting Power-Up (5 minutes)

1 Minute Power Pose

2 Minutes Reviewing Talking Points

2 Minutes Visualizing Successful Outcomes

5. Post-Meeting Reset (5 minutes)

- Document Key Contributions
- Plan Follow-Up Actions
- Reset Energy with Deep Breathing

6. Afternoon Energy Maintenance

- Strategic Breaks Every 90 minutes
- Movement Between Meetings
- Hydration & Nutrition Plan

Daily Practice for Rewiring Confidence

1. Achievements Review

- Read Yesterday's Wins
- Set Today's Intention
- Review Long-Term Vision

2. Power Statement Recitation

- Personal Value Proposition
- Key Accomplishments
- Core Strengths

3. Visualization Exercise

- Successful Meeting Interactions
- Confident Communication
- Positive Feedback Scenarios

Evening Reinforcement to Reset & Refuel

1. Success Documentation

- Record Daily Wins
- Note Positive InteractionsDocument Progress & Impact

2. Growth Recognition

- Identify Learning Moments
- Plan Tomorrow's Opportunities

- Celebrate Progress

3. System Reset

- Release Any Negative Interactions
- Set New Positive Intentions

Weekly Integration Practices

Sunday Strategy Session

- Review Previous Week
- Plan Coming Week
- Set Specific Intentions

Friday Look Back Session

- Success Review & Weekly Wins
- Course Correction
- Celebration Practice

Monthly Mastery Techniques

- Review Confidence Growth
- Strategy Refinement
- Update & Refresh Any Limiting Beliefs and Adjust Energy Management Techniques
- Refine Communication Approaches

Power Move Challenge

Alright, power players, I'm giving you a two-part challenge:

First, choose one of the following strategies to begin implementing:

1. The Presence Protocol for your next three meetings

2. Start your Visibility Portfolio

3. Begin your daily Peak Performance and Confidence practice

Second, find an ally, someone else who's dealing with similar challenges, and share this information with them so that you hold each other accountable for implementing these strategies.

Remember, you're not just doing this for yourself. Every time you speak up, stand firm and succeed, you're making it easier for the next generation of women in your field. Your presence matters, your voice matters, and your success matters. Empowerment isn't a destination; it's a journey. Stay resilient, stay secure, and let's continue building a future where everyone's voice matters.

CHAPTER EIGHT

THE POWER OF DIGITAL CREDENTIALS

"Education is the passport to the future, for tomorrow belongs to those who prepare for it today."

~Malcolm X

The meeting room fell silent as I walked in, my laptop tucked under my arm, credentials displayed prominently on the badge around my neck: "Dr. Cheryl Cooper, CISSP, CISM." In that moment, I felt the weight of not just being a cybersecurity expert but a Black woman in a sea of predominantly white male faces. The credentials on my badge weren't just letters, they were my right to be there, earned through years of dedication to continuous learning.

If you're a woman of color pursuing a career in cybersecurity, you must understand the strategic role education will play in helping you advance in your career. This chapter provides insight into how to leverage your educational credentials to protect against bias and overcome barriers to advancement. The experiences shared will underscore why continuous learning is an unassailable foundation for your career.

In the rapidly evolving landscape of cybersecurity, credentials and continuous learning serve as critical access points to career advancement and professional recognition for all women, particularly for Black women in technology. While technical skills are fundamental, the journey to success in cybersecurity often requires more than just practical knowledge. Formal credentials help to validate your expertise and can be transformative in opening doors that might otherwise remain closed.

A Personal Reflection in Time

I often marvel internally at how education has played a role in helping me maintain a sense of normalcy in the world. I have a bachelor's degree, two master's degrees, a host of industry certifications, and a Ph.D. Somehow, by God's grace, I managed to achieve so much professional success despite struggling with alcohol abuse, depression, and long bouts of PTSD.

After leaving the military, I earned a Bachelor of Arts in Management and Human Relations while working for a Fortune 500 telecommunications company.

Although I had a bachelor's degree, I was still learning how to apply my classroom learning to real-world work experiences. I then decided to pursue a Master's in Business Administration. Shortly after receiving my MBA, I was promoted to supervisor and later to a management role.

I then felt a strong desire to go back to school to obtain a master's in criminal justice with an emphasis on cybersecurity. At the time, I believed an additional educational degree would help open up more leadership opportunities for me at the company I worked for. Perhaps even a position in a different department where I could expand my skills and responsibilities. And I was right. As I grew as a leader, so did my confidence and belief in my ability to achieve even greater success. Before I knew it, I was visualizing myself with a Ph.D., I mean, why not?

Having a doctorate would be another tool to help me reach even higher heights in my field. I also felt that earning my Ph.D. allowed me to rewrite my story. I had already beaten the odds, and my past was in my rearview. I had no intention of erasing it, and I now had the power to author new chapters that reflected who I had become despite the many life hurdles I endured and overcame. I was less foolish, more mature, wiser, bold, beautiful, competent, and brilliant. By this time, I had witnessed how advanced degrees helped propel others in my field, and I was ready to open new doors, be more impactful, and make a difference.

While studying to earn my Ph.D., I worked full-time as a cybersecurity risk manager and raised my young daughter. One evening, after spending hours working on my dissertation, she found me asleep at my desk. Instead of seeing exhaustion, she saw inspiration. "Mom," she said. "Watching you study makes me believe I can do anything." That moment reminded me that our educational journeys impact more than just our own careers; they light the way for others. Seeing my little girl so proud of me, I was determined to finish, and I did. I earned my doctorate in computer science, and my daughter sat front and center at my graduation to watch me as I walked across the stage and be hooded.

The "Good Old Boy" Network vs. Educational Currency

Earning my Ph.D. mattered. Let me share a story that illustrates why credentials matter so much for women of color. Early in my career, a less qualified male colleague was promoted over me to a senior security position.

At the time, I was super happy for him. I even joined the team after work to celebrate his promotion. During a congratulatory toast, he candidly admitted, "I got the heads-up about the role during a golf game with Steve (the Chief Technology Officer)." That moment crystallized something I had long suspected. While some of us can rely on informal networks, I needed something more concrete as a Black woman.

The "good old boy" network—an informal system of connections and relationships often built through shared backgrounds, social clubs, and generational ties—continues to influence technological career advancement. While many White professionals can leverage these established networks for opportunities, minorities aren't typically members of these elite, invisible but powerful circles. This stark reality creates an uneven playing field that often requires people of color to present impeccable credentials to receive the same opportunities that others might access through informal channels.

According to a 2023 LinkedIn workplace study:

- 85% of All Jobs are Filled Through Networking
- 73% of White Professionals Report having Strong Professional Networks

- Only 48% of Black Professionals Report Having Strong Professional Networks

- For Black Women in Technology, the Number Drops to 32%

Minorities in cybersecurity are navigating an industry where representation remains limited and traditional networking channels—often built on historical relationships and shared backgrounds—are less accessible. This reality makes our educational achievements not just qualifications but essential keys to unlocking opportunities others might access through informal networks.

The Power of Educational Empowerment

In 2023, I attended a cybersecurity conference where I was scheduled to present my research on zero-trust architecture. During the Q & A session, a male attendee challenged my methodology. I calmly walked him through my credentials, my years of practical experience, my relevant certifications, and my doctoral research in the area. The dynamic shifted immediately. This wasn't an isolated incident. It's a pattern many women (especially women of color) in technology face.

A fellow Black woman colleague in cybersecurity shared her personal story with me after we became more acquainted. Despite having ten years of hands-on experience, she was passed over for a CISO position in favor of a White male with fewer years in the field but an MBA from a prestigious university. This motivated her to pursue both her CISSP and her own executive MBA. Two years later, she secured a CISO position at a larger company. When she called to share the news, she said boldly, "My credentials became my equalizer."

The Leadership Gap: A Closer Look

Recent studies paint a clear picture of the leadership disparity. According to Forrester, women hold only 24% of Cybersecurity Leadership Roles.

At Fortune 500 companies:

- Only 4.4% Have Women CEOs
- 8.2% Have Women CIOs
- 4.3% Have Women CISOs

This same research shows Black women hold less than 1% of technology executive positions. This disparity means education for Black women is more than personal development. Each degree, certification, and qualification serve as validation that cannot be easily dismissed. Meanwhile, Black women with advanced degrees still often earn much less than their white counterparts (male or female) with the same or similar credentials.

The Continuous Learning Imperative

In cybersecurity, the landscape shifts daily. New threats emerge, technologies evolve, and methodologies advance. This reality makes continuous learning not just advisable but essential. Each new certification, each advanced course, and each additional credential becomes another data point validating your expertise. In a field where Black women are often subjected to additional scrutiny, maintaining an educational advance, whether fair or not, is vital.

5 Key Takeaways

1. Educational credentials serve as non-negotiable validation in spaces where informal networks might be less accessible.

2. Advanced degrees and certifications can help level the playing field in an industry where representation remains limited.

3. Continuous learning is both a professional necessity and a strategic advantage.

4. The journey to advanced credentials, while challenging, builds resilience and expertise that enhance leadership capabilities.

5. Educational achievements create opportunities for mentorship and open doors for future generations.

Action Steps for Readers

1. Audit Your Educational Portfolio

- Review Your Current Credentials

- Identify Gaps in Your Educational Background

- Research Programs and Certifications that Align with Your

- Career Goals

- Create a Timeline for Pursuing Additional Credentials

2. Develop a Continuous Learning Strategy

- Subscribe to Leading Cybersecurity Journals and Publications

- Join Professional Organizations in Your Specialty Area

- Set Aside Time Each Week to Learning New Skills

- Document Your Learning Journey and Achievements

3. Build Your Support Network

- Network t with Other Black Women in Technology

- Seek Mentors Who Have Achieved Similar Educational Goals

- Join Study Groups or Create Learning Cohorts
- Share Your Knowledge by Mentoring Others

4. Create Your Credential Roadmap

- List Certifications Most Valued for Your Target Role
- Research Requirements for Each Credential
- Develop a Budget for Educational Investments
- Set Specific Timelines for Achieving Credentials

5. Leverage Your Achievements

- Update Your Professional Profiles
- Share Your Expertise via Speaking Engagements or Publications

6. Document Your Journey

- Keep a "Credentials Diary"
- Track Instances When Your Credentials Made a Difference

7. Build Your Personal Brand

- Create Content Showcasing Your Expertise
- Seek Speaking Opportunities at Conferences and Tech Forums
- Publish Articles in Industry Publications

Your continuous learning journey can create a legacy of excellence that challenges stereotypes and opens doors for those who will follow. In cybersecurity, we protect systems from threats. Through education and achievement, we protect our right to be in the rooms where decisions are made.

Chapter Nine

Coding Your Future: Essential Tech Skills

"The only way to do great work is to love what you do."

~Steve Jobs

It's 2:00 AM, and I'm deep into a virtual cybersecurity testing exercise. My fingers dance across the keyboard as I navigate a simulated network. Of course, I'm not at the office at this time. I'm in my spare bedroom, which I've transformed into a personal cybersecurity playground where bits and bytes come alive and digital fortresses are built and breached.

As I take a moment to stretch and sip my now-cold coffee, I can't help but smile at how far I've come from my first fumbling attempts at coding. My home lab is a hodgepodge of repurposed computers and virtual machines. It has been my training ground, my battlefield, and my sanctuary. The place where I've honed my skills, made countless mistakes, and experienced those exhilarating "aha!" moments that every tech enthusiast lives for.

In this chapter, you'll learn the essential technical skills that form the foundation of a successful cybersecurity career. But more than that, we're going to dive into the world of home labs and how to build your own cyber-dojo where theory meets practice, and you can unleash your inner hacker (ethically, of course) without fear of breaking anything important.

Whether you're a complete novice or a seasoned IT professional looking to pivot into cybersecurity, understanding the core technical skills and having a space to practice them empowers you to take control of your learning journey. By the end of this chapter, you'll have a clear roadmap of the skills you need to develop and the knowledge to set up your very own cybersecurity lab.

The Importance of Entry-Level Certifications

Let's start with a crucial stepping stone as you kickstart your cybersecurity journey: entry-level certifications.

Entry-level certifications validate foundational knowledge of your technical skills and can significantly boost your chances of landing a good cybersecurity junior role. In the industry, the

CompTIA Security+ certification stands out as the most requested entry-level cybersecurity certification on job postings. This certification covers various security concepts, from network security and cryptography to risk management and incident response.

Why is CompTIA Security+ so valuable for beginners?

1. **Industry Recognition:** It's widely recognized and respected, making it a valuable addition to your resume.

2. **Broad Knowledge Base:** It covers a wide range of security topics, giving you a solid foundation in various aspects of cybersecurity.

3. **DoD Approved:** The U.S. Department of Defense has approved it to meet directive 8570.01-M requirements, making it particularly valuable for those interested in government or defense-related cybersecurity roles.

4. **Vendor-Neutral:** Unlike certifications tied to specific technologies, Security+ provides a vendor-neutral perspective, making your skills more broadly applicable.

5. **Prerequisite for Advanced Certifications:** It often serves as a stepping stone to more advanced certifications, setting you up for long-term career growth.

Preparing for the Security+ exam can also guide your initial learning in cybersecurity. The topics covered in the exam align well with the essential skills we'll discuss in this chapter, making your certification preparation and skill development a synergistic process.

The Cybersecurity Tech Toolkit

Just as an expert chef needs to know their knives, a cybersecurity professional must be familiar with various technical tools and concepts. Let's walk through some of the key skills you should focus on developing:

1. **Networking Fundamentals:** Understanding how networks function is crucial. This includes being knowledgeable about TCP/IP (Transmission Control Protocol/Internet Protocol)

- DNS (Domain Name System)
- VPNs (Virtual Private Networks)
- Network topologies

I remember when I first grasped how packets move across a network. It was like seeing the Matrix code for the first time. Suddenly, the invisible world of data flow became visible to me.

2. **Operating Systems:** Familiarity with Windows, Linux, and macOS is important. You should be comfortable navigating and securing these systems. Key areas to focus on include:

- Command-line Interfaces (CLI)
- System Administration
- Security Features

Don't be intimidated by the command line; embrace it. I still remember the thrill of successfully running my first bash script.

3. **Programming and Scripting:** While you don't need to be a software developer, basic programming skills can be incredibly useful. Focus on:

- Python
- JavaScript
- PowerShell

As national security research expert Daniel Miessler notes, "The difference between good and great in security is often the ability to code." [^1]

4. **Database Management:** Understanding databases and basic SQL knowledge are important for many cybersecurity roles. Key concepts include:

- Relational database structures
- Basic SQL queries
- Database security principles

5. **Cloud Security:** As more organizations move to the cloud, understanding platforms like AWS, Azure, or Google Cloud becomes increasingly valuable. Focus on:

- Cloud architecture basics
- Shared responsibility models
- Cloud-specific security controls and best practices

6. **Virtualization:** Knowledge of virtual machines and containerization is crucial for many cybersecurity tasks. Key areas include:

- Hypervisors (VMware or VirtualBox)
- Containerization technologies (Docker)
- Security implications of virtualization

7. **Cryptography:** Understanding encryption methods and practices is fundamental to protecting data. Key concepts include:

- Symmetric vs. asymmetric encryption
- Hashing functions
- Digital signatures and certificates

8. **Web Application Security:** Familiarity with common web vulnerabilities and how to protect against them is essential in today's web-centric world. Focus on:

- OWASP Top 10 vulnerabilities

- Web application firewalls

- Secure coding practices

Remember, you don't need to master all these skills simultaneously. Start with the basics and build your knowledge over time. The key is maintaining a curiosity for learning and a willingness to explore new technologies.

The Power of a Home Lab

Now, let's talk about one of the most effective ways to develop these skills: Building your own home cybersecurity lab. Think of this as creating your personal tech training ground where you can practice techniques, test theories, and learn by doing, all in a safe and controlled environment.

When I first started in cybersecurity, I was intimidated by setting up my own lab. It seemed like something only seasoned professionals or large organizations could do. But I quickly realized that with some basic hardware and free software, I could create a powerful learning environment right in my own home.

Top 5 Home Lab Benefits

1. **Safe Environment for Experimentation:** In your lab, you can experiment with different tools and techniques without the risk of affecting production systems or violating any laws or ethical guidelines.

2. **Hands-On Learning:** There's no substitute for hands-on experience. As security expert Kevin Mitnick said, "You can't just read about it; you've got to roll up your sleeves and do it."

3. **Skill Validation:** A lab allows you to validate your skills and knowledge in a practical setting, which is crucial for job interviews and certifications.

4. **Portfolio Building:** The projects you complete in your lab can become part of your professional portfolio, demonstrating your skills to potential employers.

5. **Continuous Learning:** With your own lab, you can keep pace with the rapidly evolving cybersecurity landscape, always having a place to test new tools and techniques.

Setting Up Your First Cyber Lab

Now that you understand the importance of creating a home lab let's dive into how to set one up. Don't worry if you're on a tight budget. There are options for every financial situation.

Selecting the Right Hardware

1. **Dedicated Hardware:** If you have the space and budget, setting up a dedicated machine for your lab would be ideal. This could be an old desktop computer or a small form factor PC.

2. **Virtual Machines on Your Main Computer:** If you're short on space or funds, you can set up virtual machines on your main computer using software like VirtualBox or VMware Workstation Player (both have free versions).

3. **Raspberry Pi:** These tiny, affordable computers are great for learning Linux and networking concepts.

Optimal Software Essentials

1. **Virtualization Software:** VirtualBox or VMware Workstation Player for creating and managing virtual machines.

2. **Operating Systems:** Download free versions of Windows and various Linux distributions (Ubuntu, Kali Linux, CentOS).

3. **Security Tools:** Many essential cybersecurity tools are open-source and free, such as Wireshark for network analysis, Metasploit for penetration testing, and OSSEC for intrusion detection.

4. **Programming Environments:** Install Python, set up a web server, and get familiar with command-line interfaces.

Lab Projects to Get Started:

1. **Network Mapping:** Use tools like Nmap to map your home network.

2. **Vulnerability Scanning:** Set up intentionally vulnerable systems like Metasploitable and begin to practice identifying vulnerabilities.

3. **Web Application Security:** Deploy an intentionally vulnerable web application like DVWA (Damn Vulnerable Web Application) and practice identifying and exploiting common web vulnerabilities.

4. **Forensics Practice:** Create disk images and practice digital forensics techniques.

5. **Scripting Challenges:** Write scripts to automate common security tasks, like log analysis or system hardening.

Remember, the key is to start small and gradually expand your lab as your skills and interests grow. Don't be afraid to break things; that's often when the best learning happens.

5-Part Challenge

As we wrap up this chapter, I want to challenge you to take five new steps if you haven't already on your tech and cybersecurity journey:

1. **Set Up A Personal Home Lab:** Get your lab up and running, whether it's a virtual machine on your current computer or a dedicated system.

2. **Choose A Project:** Pick one of the lab projects we discussed and dive in. Don't worry about getting it perfect. The goal is to start learning by doing.

3. **Join An Online Community:** Find online forums or local meetups where you can share your experiences, ask questions, and learn from others on similar journeys.

4. **Document Your Progress:** Keep a blog or journal of your lab experiences. This will help reinforce your learning and serve as a portfolio of your skills.

5. **Start Preparing for the CompTIA Security+ Exam:** Begin studying for this valuable entry-level certification alongside your practical lab work.

Key Points Summary

1. Essential technical skills for cybersecurity include networking, operating systems, programming, database management, cloud security, virtualization, cryptography, and web application security.

2. The CompTIA Security+ certification is a valuable entry-level credential for aspiring cybersecurity professionals.

3. A home cybersecurity lab provides a safe environment for hands-on learning, skill validation, and continuous improvement.

4. A home lab can be set up with minimal resources, using virtual machines, old hardware, or even a Raspberry Pi.

5. Practical projects in your lab, such as network mapping, vulnerability scanning, and forensics practice, are crucial for skill development.

6. Continuous learning and adaptation are key in the ever-evolving field of cybersecurity.

Remember, every expert was once a beginner. The most important step is to start.

CHAPTER TEN

BUILDING YOUR CYBERSECURITY COMMAND CENTER

"A home lab is not just a space; it's a sanctuary for curiosity and innovation. It's where the mind can wander, and the heart can grow in knowledge, especially for women in cybersecurity."

~*DarkCybe*

It's time to walk through setting up your first home lab. Don't worry if you're starting from scratch; this chapter will teach you nine essential steps to building your own Cybersecurity Command Center.

Step 1: Choose Your Hardware

You don't need a supercomputer to start. Here's what you should aim for:

- A computer with at least 8GB of RAM (16GB or more is better)
- A multi-core processor (Intel i5/i7 or AMD Ryzen 5/7)
- At least 256GB of storage (SSD preferred for faster performance)

If you're using a laptop, ensure it has good cooling, as virtualization can be resource-intensive.

Step 2: Set Up Virtualization Software

Virtualization allows you to run multiple operating systems on a single physical machine. We'll use Oracle VirtualBox, which is free and user-friendly.

1. Go to https://www.virtualbox.org/
2. Click on "Download VirtualBox 6.1" (or the latest version)
3. Choose your host operating system (Windows, macOS, or Linux)
4. Download and install the software, following the on-screen instructions

Step 3: Install Your Base Operating System

Start with Ubuntu, a user-friendly Linux distribution.

1. Go to https://ubuntu.com/download/desktop

2. Download the latest LTS (Long Term Support) version

3. Open VirtualBox and click "New"

4. Name your virtual machine (e.g., "Ubuntu Lab"), select "Linux" as the type, and "Ubuntu" as the version

5. Allocate at least 2GB of RAM and create a virtual hard disk (VDI, dynamically allocated, at least 20GB)

6. Once created, select your new VM and click "Settings"

7. Under "Storage," click on "Empty" under "Controller: IDE"

8. Click the disk icon next to "Optical Drive" and choose "Choose a disk file"

9. Select the Ubuntu ISO you downloaded

10. Click "OK" to save settings

11. Start the VM and follow the Ubuntu installation instructions

Step 4: Add More Operating Systems

Repeat the process in Step 3 to create additional virtual machines:

1. Windows 10:

- Download Windows 10 ISO from Microsoft's website

- Create a new VM in VirtualBox, selecting "Windows 10" as the version

- Allocate at least 4GB of RAM and 50GB of storage

2. Kali Linux:

- Download Kali Linux from https://www.kali.org/downloads/

- Create a new VM, selecting "Debian" as the version
- Allocate at least 2GB of RAM and 20GB of storage

Step 5: Set Up a Virtual Network

VirtualBox allows you to create isolated networks for your VMs:

1. In VirtualBox, go to File > Preferences > Network
2. Click on the "+" icon to add a new NAT Network
3. Name it "Cyber Lab Network" and ensure "Enable Network" is checked
4. Click "OK" to save

Now, for each of your VMs:

1. Go to Settings > Network
2. For "Attached to," select "NAT Network"
3. In the "Name" dropdown, select "Cyber Lab Network"
4. Click "OK" to save

This setup allows your VMs to communicate with each other but keeps them isolated from your host machine and the internet.

Step 6: Install Security Tools

Here's a step-by-step script to help you set up and install security tools on a Kali Linux VM:

1. Download and Install Virtualization Software

- VMware Workstation/Player or VirtualBox: Download and install your preferred virtualization software from their official websites.

2. Download Kali Linux ISO

- Visit the Kali Linux official website and download the latest ISO file.

3. Create a New Virtual Machine

VMware:

1. Open VMware and select "Create a New Virtual Machine."
2. Choose "Installer disc image file (iso)" and browse to the Kali Linux ISO.
3. Follow the prompts to configure the VM settings (e.g., memory, CPU, disk space).

VirtualBox:

1. Open VirtualBox and click "New."
2. Name your VM and select "Linux" and "Debian (64-bit)".
3. Allocate memory and create a virtual hard disk.
4. Select "Use an existing virtual hard disk file" and browse to the Kali Linux ISO.

4. Install Kali Linux

Start the VM and follow the installation prompts:

1. Select "Graphical Install."
2. Choose your language, location, and keyboard layout.
3. Configure the network settings and set up a user account.
4. Partition the disk (guided partitioning is recommended for beginners).
5. Complete the installation and reboot the VM.

5. Update and Upgrade Kali Linux

- Open a terminal and run the following commands to update and upgrade your system:

- sudo apt update

- sudo apt full-upgrade -y

6. Install VMware Tools or VirtualBox Guest Additions

VMware:

1. Install open-vm-tools:

- sudo apt install open-vm-tools-desktop -y

- sudo reboot

- VirtualBox:

2. Insert Guest Additions CD Image from the VirtualBox menu.

3. Mount the CD image and run the installer:

- sudo mkdir /mnt/cdrom

- sudo mount /dev/cdrom /mnt/cdrom

- sudo /mnt/cdrom/VBoxLinuxAdditions.run

- sudo reboot

7. Install Essential Security Tools

Nmap: Network scanning tool.

sudo apt install nmap -y

Metasploit Framework: Penetration testing framework.

sudo apt install metasploit-framework -y

Wireshark: Network protocol analyzer.

sudo apt install wireshark -y

John the Ripper: Password cracking tool.

sudo apt install john -y

Burp Suite: Web vulnerability scanner.

sudo apt install burpsuite -y

8. Set Up Your Virtual Network

- Configure network settings in your VM to simulate different network environments. You can use tools like GNS3 or Cisco Packet Tracer for advanced network simulations.

9. Explore and Practice

- Start exploring the tools and practicing your skills in your new cyber lab. Use online resources, tutorials, and practice labs to enhance your learning.

Following these steps will install a fully functional Kali Linux VM with essential security tools. This means you are ready to start your cybersecurity journey. Happy hacking (ethically, of course).

Basic Security Exercises

Now that your lab is set up try these beginner-friendly activities to practice your skills:

1. Set up a web server on Ubuntu:

- In your Ubuntu VM, open a terminal
- Install Apache: `sudo apt install apache2`
- Start the service: `sudo systemctl start apache2`
- Get the IP address: `ip addr show`

2. Access the web server from Windows:

- In your Windows VM, open a web browser
- Enter the IP address of your Ubuntu VM

3. Use Wireshark to capture traffic:

- In your Kali Linux VM, open Wireshark
- Select the network interface and start capturing
- In another VM, browse to a website
- Stop the capture and analyze the traffic

4. Scan your network with Nmap:

- In your Kali Linux VM, open a terminal
- Run: `sudo nmap -sn <network-address>/24`(Replace <network-address> with your NAT network address, e.g., 10.0.2.0/24)

Important Notes for Beginners

As you embark on your home lab journey, always keep these four important points in mind:

1. Never use tools or techniques you learn on systems you don't own or have explicit permission to test.

2. Keep your lab virtual machines isolated from your home network and the internet unless necessary for a specific learning activity.

3. Regularly update and patch your virtual machines as you would with real systems.

4. Remember that tools like Metasploit can be dangerous if misused. Always practice responsible and ethical behavior.

Learning Resources for Your Cyber Journey

You'll likely have questions or need guidance as you build and explore your home lab. Here are some excellent resources for beginners:

1. Online Courses:

- Coursera: "Introduction to Cyber Security Specialization" by NYU

- edX: "Cybersecurity Fundamentals" by RITx

- Cybrary: "CompTIA Security+ Certification Prep"

2. YouTube Tutorials:

- "NetworkChuck": Offers engaging, beginner-friendly cybersecurity content

- "John Hammond": Provides in-depth tutorials on various cybersecurity topics

- "David Bombal": Covers a wide range of networking and cybersecurity topics

3. Recommended Books:

- "The Web Application Hacker's Handbook" by Dafydd Stuttard and Marcus Pinto

- "Penetration Testing: A Hands-On Introduction to Hacking" by Georgia Weidman

- "CompTIA Security+ Get Certified Get Ahead: SY0-601 Study Guide" by Darril Gibson

4. Capture The Flag (CTF) Challenges:

- HackTheBox: Offers a range of challenges for different skill levels

- TryHackMe: Provides guided, gamified learning experiences

- PicoCTF: Designed for beginners, with a focus on high school and college students

5. Official Documentation:

- VirtualBox User Manual: https://www.virtualbox.org/manual/

- Ubuntu Documentation: https://help.ubuntu.com/

- Kali Linux Documentation: https://www.kali.org/docs/

6. Cybersecurity News and Blogs:

- Krebs on Security: https://krebsonsecurity.com/

- Dark Reading: https://www.darkreading.com/

- The Hacker News: https://thehackernews.com/

Building your technical skills is a journey, not a destination. The field of cybersecurity is constantly evolving, so cultivate a mindset of lifelong learning. Your home lab is just the beginning, a safe space to explore, make mistakes, and grow your skills.

Advancing Your Lab and Skills

As you become more comfortable with your basic lab setup, consider these advanced steps to further develop your skills:

1. **Add Vulnerable Machines:** Install purposely vulnerable systems like Metasploitable or DVWA (Damn Vulnerable Web Application) to practice ethical hacking techniques.

2. **Explore Different Networking Setups:** Experiment with different network configurations in VirtualBox, such as bridged adapters or host-only networking.

3. **Implement Security Controls:** Set up firewalls, intrusion detection systems, and log management tools to create a more realistic environment.

4. **Practice Incident Response:** Simulate cyber-attacks in your lab and practice detecting, containing, and mitigating them.

5. **Explore Cloud Security:** Set up free-tier accounts on cloud platforms like AWS or Azure to understand cloud infrastructure and security.

The Importance of Hands-on Experience

While theoretical knowledge is important, hands-on experience is crucial in cybersecurity. Your home lab provides a safe, legal environment to apply what you've learned and develop practical skills. Here's why this is so important:

1. **Real-world Application:** Theory comes to life when you apply it in practice. Your lab allows you to see how concepts work in real (virtual) environments.

2. **Problem-solving Skills:** Troubleshooting issues in your lab develops critical thinking and problem-solving skills essential in cybersecurity roles.

3. **Confidence Building:** As you successfully complete projects and overcome challenges in your lab, you'll build confidence in your abilities.

4. **Prepare for Certification Exams**: Many cybersecurity certifications include practical components. Your lab experience will be invaluable in preparing for these exams.

5. **Portfolio Development:** Document your lab projects to create a portfolio showcasing your skills to potential employers.

Balancing Technical Skills with Soft Skills

While this chapter focused primarily on technical skills, remember successful cybersecurity professionals also need strong soft skills. As you develop your technical abilities, don't neglect these equally crucial areas:

1. **Mastering Communications:** The ability to explain complex technical concepts to non-technical stakeholders is crucial. I've seen brilliant technicians struggle in their careers because they couldn't effectively communicate their ideas to management or clients.

2. **The Art of Teamwork:** Cybersecurity often involves collaborating with diverse teams across an organization. As

security expert Bruce Schneier notes, "Security is a team sport."

3. **Being Adaptable:** The rapid pace of technological change requires a willingness to learn and adapt continuously. What's cutting-edge today may be obsolete tomorrow.

4. **Critical Thinking:** The ability to analyze complex situations and make sound decisions is essential in cybersecurity. This skill often differentiates between a good analyst and a great one.

5. **Ethical Judgment:** Understanding and adhering to ethical standards is paramount in cybersecurity. Our ethical responsibilities grow proportionately as we gain more power to access and manipulate data.

Continuing Your Journey: Beyond the Home Lab

As you become more comfortable with your home lab and the basic skills we've discussed, remember that this is just the beginning of your cybersecurity journey. The vast field constantly evolves, offering numerous paths for specialization and growth.

Consider exploring the following areas:

Cloud Security: As more organizations move their operations to the cloud, expertise in securing cloud environments is increasingly valuable.

- Internet of Things (IoT) Security: With the proliferation of connected devices, understanding how to secure IoT ecosystems is becoming crucial.

- Artificial Intelligence and Machine Learning in Cybersecurity: These technologies are increasingly used by both defenders and attackers.

- Blockchain and Cryptocurrency Security: As digital currencies become more mainstream, the need for professionals to understand their security implications grows.

Remember, the key to success in cybersecurity is continuous learning. As technology evolves, so too must our skills and knowledge.

Ethical Considerations in Cybersecurity

As we wrap up this chapter, I want to emphasize the importance of ethics in cybersecurity. The skills and tools we've discussed are powerful, and with that power comes great responsibility. Always use your knowledge and abilities ethically and legally. Be creative and curious, but always be responsible. The digital realm needs innovative defenders like you.

CHAPTER ELEVEN

ARTIFICIAL INTELLIGENCE IN CYBERSECURITY

"Artificial Intelligence is not just a tool but a powerful ally in the quest for cybersecurity, enhancing our ability to detect threats and respond swiftly to challenges that were once unimaginable."

~Anurag Gurtu and Damien Lim

As I sit here, surrounded by screens displaying real-time threat intelligence and automated response protocols, I can't help but marvel at how far we've come in the world of cybersecurity. When I first started in this field, the idea of machines learning to detect and respond to threats seemed like science fiction. Now, it's not just reality; it's becoming the norm. So, having a deep understanding of artificial intelligence (AI) isn't just important; it's essential for anyone entering the field.

The numbers speak for themselves. According to recent data, the use of AI in cybersecurity has seen explosive growth. Between April 2023 and January 2024, enterprise AI and machine learning transactions surged by an astounding 595%. This isn't just a trend; it's a seismic shift in how we approach cybersecurity. It's changing how we detect threats, respond to incidents, and predict future attacks. AI is also rapidly enhancing our ability to protect systems and data in previously impossible ways.

Here are just a few ways AI has already changed the game:

1. **Enhanced Detection Capabilities:** AI systems can analyze vast amounts of data faster and more accurately than human analysts, identifying potential threats that might go unnoticed.

2. **Proactive Threat Response:** AI doesn't just detect threats; it predicts and responds to them automatically, reducing the need for human intervention in many cases.

3. **Efficient Resource Management:** By automating routine tasks, AI frees human cybersecurity professionals to focus on more complex, strategic work.

When I started working with AI-powered security tools, I was amazed at how quickly they could identify patterns in network traffic that would have taken me hours or even days to spot. Nowadays, it's like having a tireless, incredibly observant assistant working alongside me 24/7.

Here are some helpful AI starters:

1. **Familiarize Yourself with AI-powered Tools:** Many cybersecurity platforms now incorporate AI. Get hands-on experience with these tools through your work, in a home lab, or online learning platforms.

2. **Stay Informed:** AI in tech and cybersecurity is evolving rapidly. Make it a habit to read industry news, follow thought leaders on social media, and attend webinars or conferences when possible.

3. **Develop Relevant AI Skills:** While you don't need to be an AI expert, being skilled in data analysis, programming (especially Python), and statistics will serve you well in working with AI systems.

4. **Consider Certification:** As AI becomes more prevalent in cybersecurity, certifications are emerging that focus on this intersection. Keep an eye out for these opportunities to boost your knowledge.

Threat Detection and Prevention

One of AI's most powerful cybersecurity applications is in threat detection and prevention. AI systems can analyze network traffic patterns, user behavior, and system logs at a scale and speed that would be impossible for human analysts alone. These systems use advanced machine learning techniques to identify real-time anomalies and potential threats, significantly enhancing an organization's security posture.

For example, I worked with a financial institution implementing an AI-powered threat detection system. Within the first month, the system identified a subtle, ongoing data exfiltration attempt that had been going on for weeks, completely undetected by traditional security measures.

AI detected minute anomalies in data transfer patterns consistent across multiple user accounts, which would have been almost impossible for a human analyst to piece together.

AI-powered systems also predict potential vulnerabilities before they're exploited. Analyzing vast amounts of threat intelligence data at warp speed, these systems foresee patterns that suggest where attackers might strike next, allowing security teams to proactively strengthen defenses.

Automated Incident Response

Another exciting application of AI is automated incident response. When a security incident occurs, every second counts. AI systems are initiating response protocols instantly, containing threats before they spread.

For example, I worked on a case where a ransomware attack hit a healthcare provider. Their AI-powered security system detected the initial encryption attempts, immediately isolated the affected systems, and began backing up critical data, all before the human security team was even alerted. This AI rapid response prevented what could have been a catastrophic data loss.

User and Entity Behavior Analytics (UEBA)

AI is also revolutionizing how we approach insider threats through User and Entity Behavior Analytics (UEBA). These systems create baseline profiles of normal behavior for users and entities within a network. Any deviation from these baselines can trigger alerts or automated responses.

In one organization I worked with, the UEBA system flagged unusual activity on a senior executive's account. It turned out that a sophisticated attacker had compromised the account and was slowly escalating privileges.

The AI system noticed this behavior pattern long before it became apparent through traditional monitoring.

The Dark Side: How Cybercriminals are Leveraging AI

While AI is a powerful tool for defense, it's crucial to understand that cybercriminals are also harnessing its power to counter them effectively.

AI-Powered Phishing Attacks

One of the most concerning developments is using AI in phishing attacks. Traditional phishing emails were often easy to spot due to poor grammar, generic greetings, or obvious scam content. However, AI-powered phishing is changing the game. Cybercriminals are now using AI to:

1. Generate highly personalized phishing emails by scraping social media and other public data sources.

2. Create convincing fake websites that mimic legitimate ones, adapting in real-time to avoid detection.

3. Craft persuasive text that mimics the writing style of trusted contacts.

I recently encountered a case where an AI-generated phishing campaign targeted a company's finance department. The emails were eerily personalized, mentioning recent projects and using company-specific jargon.

Cybercriminals leveraged AI to collect publicly available company information and social media posts to create messages sent to employees that were indistinguishable from legitimate internal communications.

Intelligent Malware

AI is also being used to create more sophisticated malware. This "intelligent malware" can:

1. Adapt to avoid detection by traditional antivirus software.

2. Learn from failed attempts and improve its attack strategies.

3. Mimic normal system behavior to avoid triggering security alerts.

In one particularly alarming case, we encountered a piece of malware that used machine learning algorithms to study the behavior of the antivirus software protecting a network. It would test different techniques, learn from the responses, and adapt its behavior to remain undetected.

Automated Vulnerability Discovery

Cybercriminals are also using AI to automate the process of finding vulnerabilities in systems and applications. These AI systems can:

1. Scan vast amounts of code much faster than human hackers.

2. Identify subtle patterns that might indicate a vulnerability.

3. Generate and test exploit code automatically. (10)

The use of AI as "offensive security" presents a significant challenge. It means vulnerabilities can be discovered and exploited at machine speed, potentially outpacing human-driven patching and mitigation efforts.

Ethical Considerations in AI and Cybersecurity

As a budding cybersecurity professional, you must weigh the ethical implications associated with the use of AI, including:

AI Privacy Concerns

AI systems often require vast amounts of data to function effectively. This raises important questions about data privacy and consent. Specifically, how much personal data is it acceptable to collect and analyze in the name of security? And where do we draw the line between protection and surveillance? Companies worldwide are trying to balance the need for comprehensive monitoring with employee and consumer rights to privacy. It is a complex and complicated undertaking that will undoubtedly bring new laws and legislation.

Bias and Fairness

Believe it or not, AI systems can also inadvertently or purposefully be used to perpetuate and even amplify biases.

In cybersecurity, this could unfairly target specific ethnic groups or individuals. For example, suppose an AI system is trained on historical data where certain demographic groups were disproportionately flagged as security risks. In that case, it might continue this pattern of bias in its future predictions. As cybersecurity professionals, we are responsible for actively identifying and mitigating such biases.

Accountability and Transparency

As AI systems take on more decision-making roles in cybersecurity, questions of accountability arise. If an AI system makes a decision that leads to a security breach, who is responsible? How can we ensure that AI systems are transparent enough for their decisions to be understood and audited?

These are complex questions without easy answers and will likely be the issue you'll grapple with as you progress in your cybersecurity career.

Certifications & Skills for AI Cybersecurity Careers

1. Certified Information Systems Security Professional (CISSP): This certification is globally recognized and covers various cybersecurity topics, including risk management, network security, and software development security. It is ideal for professionals aiming to establish a strong foundation in cybersecurity.

2. Certified Ethical Hacker (CEH): This certification focuses on identifying vulnerabilities and weaknesses in systems, which is crucial for AI cybersecurity professionals who need to understand how to protect AI systems from potential threats.

3. Certified Information Security Manager (CISM): This certification is designed for individuals who manage, design, and oversee an enterprise's information security program. It benefits AI cybersecurity professionals who need to align security strategies with business goals.

4. Certified Artificial Intelligence Security Specialist (CAISS): This specialized certification focuses on the security aspects of AI systems, including threat detection, anomaly identification, and securing AI models.

5. Certified Cloud Security Professional (CCSP): As AI systems often rely on cloud infrastructure, this certification provides knowledge on securing cloud environments, which is essential for AI cybersecurity professionals.

Pursuing a career in AI cybersecurity will require a combination of certifications and skills that cover both traditional cybersecurity principles and specialized knowledge in AI and machine learning. Below is a list of basic AI skills:

1. Technical Proficiency: Expertise in various programming languages (e.g., Python, Java, C++) and familiarity with AI frameworks (e.g., TensorFlow, PyTorch) are essential for developing and securing AI systems.

2. Analytical Thinking: Strong problem-solving abilities and the capability to analyze complex security issues related to AI systems.

3. Machine Learning and AI Knowledge: Understanding machine learning algorithms, neural networks, and AI model training is crucial for identifying and mitigating security risks in AI systems.

4. Threat Intelligence and Analysis: Ability to collect, analyze, and interpret threat intelligence to predict potential attacks and formulate effective mitigation strategies.

5. Cloud Security Expertise: Skills in securing cloud environments, identifying misconfigurations, and preventing unauthorized access are vital, as AI systems often rely on cloud infrastructure.

6. Data Science: Proficiency in data science techniques to extract valuable insights from threat intelligence and build custom AI models for predictive analytics.

7. AI/ML Model Auditing: Knowledge of how AI and ML models work, including the ability to audit these models for security vulnerabilities and ensure their integrity.

The Future of AI in Cybersecurity

As we look to the future, the role of AI in cybersecurity is only set to grow. The cybersecurity AI market size was approximately $17.4 billion in 2022. It is projected to reach around $102.78 billion by the year 2032, reflecting the increasing investment and reliance on AI technologies in the cybersecurity sector.

Exciting Developments on the Horizon

1. **Quantum AI:** As quantum computing becomes a reality, it will open new possibilities for AI in cybersecurity, potentially revolutionizing encryption and threat detection.

2. **Explainable AI:** Current AI systems often operate as "black boxes," making decisions without clear explanations. Future developments in explainable AI will make understanding and trusting AI-driven security decisions easier.

3. **AI-to-AI Combat:** As defensive and offensive AI systems become more sophisticated, we may see scenarios where AI systems directly combat each other, with humans taking on more strategic and supervisory roles.

It's clear to everyone that AI is here to stay. It's at the forefront of the industry's evolution. Don't let it intimidate you; let it excite you!

CHAPTER TWELVE

HALLMARKS OF
PERSONAL BRANDING

*"Your brand is what people say about
you when you're not in the room."*

~*Jeff Bezos*

In the world of cybersecurity, we often focus on the technical aspects, including firewalls, encryption algorithms, and intrusion detection systems. However, the human element is another critical component that can make or break your career in this field. Just as a firewall protects a network, personal soft skills, and professional development can help shield and propel your career. In this chapter, we'll explore how to build your soft skills and boost your personal brand to transform you into a well-rounded tech and cybersecurity professional.

When I began my career journey in cybersecurity, I wanted to be good at everything, the go-to person. So, I made it my personal mission to learn at least the basics about every area that mattered in my field. The problem with that approach is that my energy was directed everywhere, so I was average at best. An old saying goes something like this: "Where your energy is directed, that's where your success is projected." I mean, no human can know everything about everything. So, I began switching up my approach and focusing on the areas where I thrived, which helped me eventually become exceptional at performing and speaking about my unique skills. This was a turning point in my career and set me apart in the field.

The Power of Effective Communication and Leadership

The two soft skills I chose to hone in on were communication and leadership. Early in my career, I discovered the importance of communicating my ideas effectively and leading teams confidently. I started by attending workshops, reading more books, and seeking mentors to help me master these skills. With training and a whole lot of practice, I learned to effectively tailor key messages to my audience during presentations to boost engagement and action. Being an effective communicator has been instrumental in gaining buy-in on security initiatives and building trust amongst my colleagues in the field.

Regarding leadership, I have learned that great leaders don't just dictate orders; they empower their team members, foster a culture of continuous learning, and lead by example. One of my proudest moments as a leader was mentoring a junior team member struggling with confidence. Coaching and watching her blossom into one of our most valuable security analysts taught me that leadership is not about building your personal accolades but elevating those around you.

I've also found that great leaders are great project managers and problem solvers. Managing projects efficiently requires a blend of exceptional planning, organization, and execution skills. Problem-solving, on the other hand, involves effectively and efficiently identifying issues while leveraging creativity and critical thinking to strategize potential solutions and implement the best course of action to attain desired goals. In cybersecurity, where threats are constantly evolving, possessing these leadership skills is invaluable.

I once faced a situation where my team detected an unusual pattern of data exfiltration, and our standard incident response playbook wasn't yielding results. By thinking outside the box effectively, communicating and collaborating with team members from different specialties, I successfully guided them in identifying a novel type of malware and developing a custom solution to mitigate it.

The Art of Presentation

Being a good communicator doesn't guarantee you will be a stellar presenter. Presenting is more than just being able to speak in front of an audience. It involves knowing how to structure your key messages clearly and concisely using visual aids effectively to engage and motivate your audience to act. I've found that the ability to present complex security concepts understandably and compellingly is often what separates good cybersecurity professionals from great ones.

I remember giving a presentation at a major industry conference. The topic was technical, but I made sure to include real-world examples, interactive elements, and even a bit of humor. The positive feedback I received afterward was a testament to the power of effective presentation skills in our field.

The Write Stuff: Mastering Written Communication

Written communication skills are also essential. The ability to write clear, thoughtful, and concise actionable reports can mean the difference between a vulnerability being patched or exploited. I've seen poorly written reports that led to misunderstandings and delays in addressing critical security issues. Conversely, well-written reports have helped fast-track security improvements and even secure additional budgets for crucial projects.

Building Your Cybersecurity Brand

In a competitive field like cybersecurity, it's crucial to let people know who you are, what you offer, and how you can help them. I started by identifying two soft skills that would help me build my personal brand by better showcasing the unique strengths and value I bring to the field. The soft skills you choose to focus on may differ, but identifying where you have gaps and improving in these areas can be a game-changer in your career.

For instance, I never would have had the courage to start a personal blog sharing insights on emerging cybersecurity trends and best practices had I not invested in improving my written communications and presentation skills. Over time, contributing to my blog and accepting more speaking engagements helped to establish me as a cybersecurity thought leader in my niche areas of expertise. It led to more consulting opportunities and even a book deal. Your personal brand is your professional reputation; a strong reputation in cybersecurity can open many doors.

I've built a strong personal brand by narrowing my focus and developing essential soft skills. As a result, I've achieved a level of success and fulfillment that I once thought was out of reach.

Remember, it's not about being good at everything; it's about being exceptional at what matters most to you. As you continue your journey in cybersecurity, I encourage you to view your development holistically. Technical skills are undoubtedly important, but the combination of technical expertise and well-honed soft skills will truly set you apart in this field. Cultivate the skills to help you best develop your unique personal brand.

The most effective cybersecurity professionals can bridge the gap between our field's technical and human elements. They're the ones who can explain complex threats to board members, lead diverse teams through critical incidents, and foster a culture of security awareness across entire organizations. Make sure you're well-equipped to stand out and lead forward.

Chapter Thirteen

Weaving Diversity into The Digital Tapestry

"Diversity is not about how we differ. Diversity is about embracing one another's uniqueness."

~Ola Joseph

In the ever-evolving cybersecurity landscape, diversity is not just a buzzword; it's a critical component of our collective strength. This chapter will explore the profound impact of diverse perspectives, backgrounds, and experiences on our ability to defend against cyber threats.

Our challenges are multifaceted and constantly changing in a field as dynamic and complex as cybersecurity. To effectively combat these threats, we need teams that reflect the rich tapestry of human experience and thought. Diversity brings a wealth of ideas, approaches, and solutions that a homogeneous group cannot match. Whether you're a seasoned cybersecurity expert or just starting out, understanding the value of diverse perspectives will empower you to build stronger, more innovative teams. It will also equip you with the tools to advocate for inclusive practices within your organization, fostering an environment where everyone has an equitable opportunity to thrive.

As we explore the importance of diversity in cybersecurity, you'll discover how different ways of thinking can lead to breakthroughs in solving complex problems. You'll also learn about the power of inclusive hiring practices, the role of Employee Resource Groups (ERGs), and the significance of community engagement and advocacy. Most importantly, you'll be inspired to take concrete steps towards promoting diversity and inclusion in your own career and beyond. By weaving diversity into the very fabric of our digital defenses, we can create a more resilient, innovative, and secure future for humanity.

A Moment of Pride

Standing at the podium, facing a sea of expectant faces at the annual CyberSec Summit, I couldn't help but reflect on the journey that had brought me here. The spotlights were warm on my face, starkly contrasting to the cold isolation I had felt when I first entered the industry. I took a deep breath, ready to share my story and the lessons I had learned about the power of diverse perspectives, advocacy, and community engagement in cybersecurity.

Ladies and gentlemen, I began, my voice steady despite a flutter of nerves, "Imagine a world where our digital defenses are as diverse as the threats we face. A world where our cybersecurity teams reflect the rich tapestry of human experience and thought. This isn't just a dream; it's our most powerful weapon in the fight against cyber threats."

The room fell silent, and I knew I had their attention. This was my chance to make a difference, to challenge the status quo, and to inspire change. But before I made it to this stage, I learned so many lessons about the importance of diversity in our field. For example, when I was working on a complex ransomware case, the perpetrators were always one step ahead. As the team huddled around whiteboards covered in network diagrams and code snippets, I noticed something others had overlooked. Drawing from my personal background in cultural anthropology, a field I had studied before switching to computer science, I recognized patterns in the attackers' behaviors that aligned with specific cultural practices. This insight led us to predict their next move accurately, allowing us to thwart their attack and protect our client's data. That experience was a turning point for me. It illustrated to me that diversity isn't just about having representation at the table; it's also about bringing different ways of thinking to the table. In cybersecurity, where threats constantly evolve, this diversity of thought is our secret weapon.

The road ahead won't be easy. The tech industry, particularly cybersecurity, has long been dominated by a homogeneous workforce. According to a 2021 report by (ISC)², women make up only 24% of the cybersecurity workforce, and racial minorities are significantly underrepresented. These statistics aren't just numbers; they represent missed opportunities and untapped potential.

As I continued my presentation, "Implementing inclusive hiring practices is crucial," I explained, "This means going beyond just posting job openings in diverse forums. We need to rethink and rewire our entire recruitment process."

I shared an anecdote from my time as a hiring manager at a major tech firm. Despite our best efforts, we struggled to diversify our team for many months. Then, we decided to try something different. We implemented blind resume reviews and guided structured interviewing. The results were eye-opening. We saw a significant increase in the diversity of our candidate pool and, more importantly, in the diversity of our hires. By removing identifying information from resumes and using standardized interview questions, we were able to focus on skills and potential rather than yielding to unconscious biases. But hiring is just a first step. Creating an inclusive environment where everyone feels valued and heard is equally important.

Employee Resource Groups (ERGs) can play a crucial role in this.

I vividly recall joining my company, ERG for Women in Tech, and attending the first meeting. It was the first time in my career that I felt truly seen and understood. The relief of being able to share my experiences with others who had walked a similar path was immense. Inspired by this experience, I went on to join the ERG for Black professionals in cybersecurity. The group quickly became a source of support, mentorship, and professional development for its members. But more than that, it became a catalyst for organizational change.

Through the ERG, we provided valuable insights to leadership about the challenges faced by Black employees. We organized workshops on cultural competence for the entire company and partnered with local schools to introduce students from underrepresented backgrounds to cybersecurity. "ERGs are not just support groups," I told my audience at the summit. "They are powerful agents of change. They provide a platform for underrepresented voices to be heard and for organizations to learn and grow." But our efforts can't stop at the boundaries of our own organizations. Community engagement and advocacy are crucial in creating systemic change in our industry.

I talked about my volunteer experience at a local high school, teaching an introductory course on cybersecurity. The excitement in the student's eyes when they successfully coded their first encryption algorithm was infectious. But we can't stop at inspiring the next generation. We must create pathways for them to enter and succeed in the industry. This is where partnerships with educational institutions and professional organizations become crucial, as I highlighted earlier in the book. However, our voice may be the most powerful tool in promoting diversity and inclusion. Each of us can serve as an advocate and an ally.

Allyship, I explained to my audience, helps to amplify each other's voices and create space for them to be heard. As I neared the end of my presentation, I could see that my words had resonated with many in the audience. But, I knew that inspiration without action would not create the needed change. So, I went on, "I challenge each of you to take concrete steps towards promoting diversity and inclusion in your organizations and communities. Begin implementing blind resume reviews. Start an ERG Group. Volunteer at local schools. Become allies to your underrepresented colleagues." I then provided a list of 5 practical steps that everyone in the room could take:

1. Educate yourself about the experiences of underrepresented groups.

2. Mentor someone from a different background than your own.

3. Speak up when you witness bias or discrimination.

4. Advocate for inclusive policies in your workplace.

5. Support organizations that promote diversity in tech.

"In a field as critical as cybersecurity, we can't afford to leave any talent or perspective untapped," I concluded. As I stepped away from the podium, the room erupted in applause. But the conversations that followed were more gratifying than the applause. Attendees approached me, eager to share their experiences and ideas for promoting diversity in their organizations.

I left the summit feeling energized and hopeful. I knew that change wouldn't happen overnight, but I also knew that each conversation, each ally gained while there, and each mind opened was a step in the right direction.

As I reflect on that day and the journey that led me there, I'm reminded of a quote by Verna Myers, "Diversity is being invited to the party. Inclusion is being asked to dance." In cybersecurity, we need everyone on the dance floor to bring unique moves to create a beautiful, complex, and resilient performance. Our teams, our strategies, and our solutions need to reflect the diverse society we live in. By embracing different perspectives, advocating for change, and engaging with our communities, we can make our field more inclusive and create an environment where every voice is heard, every idea is valued, and every individual feels empowered to contribute their unique strengths. That's a future worth fighting for, one byte at a time.

CHAPTER FOURTEEN

DECRYPTING TOMORROW: THE FUTURE OF CYBERSECURITY

"The future of cybersecurity is not about building higher walls, but about creating smarter defenses."

~Unknown

As I settled into my seat on the flight back from the FutureSec Conference, my mind was still buzzing with the implications of my presentation and all the things I learned. The blank pages of my notebook beckoned, and I began to jot down my thoughts on future trends and opportunities in cybersecurity. The future of cybersecurity, I wrote, is more than defending against threats; it's about shaping the digital world in which we want to live.

AI & Machine Learning

The potential of AI in cybersecurity is immense, but so are the risks. I remembered a conversation with my company's top AI researcher, Jake, after a particularly challenging security breach. "The attackers used an AI model to study our network's normal behavior," Jake explained. "They crafted their attack to mimic our normal behavior perfectly. I'm sorry, our traditional detection systems never stood a chance."

This incident was a wake-up call. We realized that to stay ahead, we needed to use AI and truly understand it. We began investing heavily in AI research, focusing on developing more robust, explainable AI models for cybersecurity. As I pondered the future of AI in tech and cybersecurity, I couldn't help but think about the rapid advancements in generative AI. Tools like ChatGPT and DALL-E had taken the world by storm, and their implications for cybersecurity were profound.

It's like playing chess against an opponent who can predict your every move, and companies need to think several steps ahead to even stay in the game. AI is here to stay, and we are just scratching the surface. Then there is quantum computing. The potential of quantum computers to break current encryption methods is also a looming threat that keeps many cybersecurity professionals up at night. I remember attending a workshop on post-quantum cryptography. The presenter, Dr. Yuki Tanaka, painted a vivid picture of both the threats and opportunities presented by quantum computing.

"Imagine a world, she said, where all of our current encryption methods are obsolete. Every encrypted message, every secure transaction from the past decades, all potentially vulnerable." The implications are staggering. But Dr. Tanaka didn't stop there.

She described the potential for quantum-resistant encryption methods and even the use of quantum principles for unbreakable communication. This is what I mean when I say ever-evolving industry and field. There is perhaps no other field that innovates faster than tech and cybersecurity.

Internet of Things (IoT) and 5G Networks

Already, the proliferation of IoT devices and the rollout of 5G networks are creating new challenges and opportunities in cybersecurity. I can't help but marvel at how our world has changed. A decade ago, a building's physical security and cybersecurity were separate concerns. Now, they were inextricably linked. As I ponder the future beyond 5G, my thoughts also turn to the emerging field of 6G technology. Although still in its early stages of development, 6G promises to revolutionize our digital landscape even further. I recently attended a conference focused on the future potential of 6G. The speaker, Dr. Amira Hassan, painted a picture of a world where digital and physical realities seamlessly merge. "6G is more than just a faster internet," Dr. Hassan explained. "It has the ability to create a network that can support truly immersive experiences, holographic communications, tactile internet, and brain-computer interfaces."

With these new advancements, the implications for cybersecurity are staggering. Imagine data transmission speeds up to 50 times faster than 5G and latency reduced to a tenth of its predecessor; 6G would enable a level of connectivity and real-time interaction we could barely comprehend. The sheer volume and velocity of data in a 6G world would require entirely new approaches to security.

In a 6G environment, we'll need to secure data and actual experiences. Just thinking about how we could protect the integrity of holographic communications blows my mind. I mean, how do we ensure the security of a brain-computer interface? The answers to these burning questions will no doubt shape the future of our field, and we need to start preparing for them now.

Cloud Security and Edge Computing

The shift to cloud computing has been one of the most significant trends in IT over the past decade, but edge computing is already emerging as a better option with its ability to process data closer to where it was generated, promising to reduce latency and bandwidth usage.

Zero Trust Architecture

The growing adoption of Zero Trust Architecture is a trend I am glad to see thrive. According to Okta's The State of Zero Trust Security 2023 report, 61% of organizations already have a Zero Trust initiative, with another 35% planning to implement one soon. This shift would create new opportunities for cybersecurity professionals skilled in identity and access management, network segmentation, and continuous monitoring.

Cybersecurity in the Post-Pandemic World

The COVID-19 pandemic has also accelerated many trends in cybersecurity, particularly around remote work and digital transformation. It is clear that these new changes, processes, and protocols adopted are also here to stay.

The Cybersecurity Talent Shortage

As you can imagine, with advancements happening rapidly, there is a growing demand for skilled cybersecurity professionals far outpacing available talent. Human Resources leaders are struggling to fill security analyst positions with qualified candidates. This unprecedented shortage is a double-edged sword. On one hand, it presents significant challenges for organizations trying to build robust security teams. On the other hand, it creates vast opportunities for those entering the tech and cybersecurity field or looking to advance their careers.

What Lies Ahead

The opportunities are truly endless for those in the field and those yet to join the ranks of today's tech and cybersecurity workforce. Regardless of where you fall on the spectrum, to stay in the game and stay ahead of the game will require constant learning, adaptation, and innovation. The full picture of the future is rapidly unfolding. There are still so many unanswered questions, but that unpredictability is what makes being in this field so magnificent. While we are unsure of what lies ahead, two things are crystal clear. Tech and Cybersecurity will never be boring, and the possibilities are endless.

CHAPTER FIFTEEN

DECODING YOUR POTENTIAL: CYBERSECURITY SKILLS INVENTORY

"Knowing yourself is the beginning of all wisdom."

~*Aristotle*

Taking stock of your skills is a crucial exercise for charting the right course for your future in cybersecurity. Until we have a more diverse tech and cybersecurity workforce, as women and minorities in these fields, we will continue to face challenges that can impact our confidence and career progression. Therefore, having a clear understanding of our capabilities will help ensure we approach any challenge from a position of strength.

So, whether you want to advance your skills or apply for a new promotion, the following skills assessment tool will help you identify and appreciate your unique talents.

Your Personal Self-Assessment Form

Instructions: Rate your proficiency in each skill area on a scale of 1 to 5.

1 = No experience 2 = Beginner 3 = Intermediate 4 = Advanced 5 = Expert

Technical Skills:

1. Network Security: _____

(Understanding firewalls, VPNs, intrusion detection systems)

2. Operating Systems: _____

(Proficiency in Windows, Linux, macOS)

3. Programming Languages: _____

(Knowledge of Python, Java, C++, etc.)

4. Web Application Security: _____

(Understanding of OWASP Top 10, web vulnerabilities)

5. Cloud Security: _____

(Familiarity securing cloud environments like AWS, Azure, Google Cloud)

6. Cryptography: _____

(Understanding encryption algorithms, key management)

7. Incident Response: _____

(Ability to detect, analyze, and mitigate security incidents)

8. Forensics: _____ (Skills in digital evidence collection and analysis)

9. Penetration Testing: _____

(Experience with ethical hacking techniques)

10. Security Information and Event Management (SIEM): _____

(Familiarity with log analysis and security event correlation)

Soft Skills:

11. Communication: _____

(Ability to explain technical concepts to non-technical audiences)

12. Problem-Solving: _____

(Analytical thinking and creative solution development)

13. Teamwork: _____

(Collaboration skills and ability to work in diverse teams)

14. Adaptability: _____

(Willingness to learn new technologies and methodologies)

15. Leadership: _____

(Ability to guide and motivate others)

16. Time Management: _____

(Skill in prioritizing tasks and meeting deadlines)

17. Ethical Decision Making: _____

(Understanding of cybersecurity ethics and legal compliance)

18. Stress Management: _____

(Ability to perform under pressure in critical situations)

19. Continuous Learning: _____

(Commitment to staying updated with the latest cybersecurity trends)

20. Cultural Competence: _____

(Understanding and respecting diverse perspectives in the workplace)

Industry Knowledge:

21. Cybersecurity Frameworks: _____

(Familiarity with NIST, ISO 27001, COBIT, etc.)

22. Regulatory Compliance: _____

(Understanding of GDPR, HIPAA, PCI DSS, etc.)

23. Threat Intelligence: _____

(Knowledge of current cyber threats and attack vectors)

24. Risk Assessment: _____

(Ability to identify and evaluate security risks)

25. Security Policies and Procedures: _____

(Experience in developing and implementing security policies)

Additional Section for Women and Minorities:

26. Confidence in Male-Dominated Environments: _____

(Comfort level in asserting yourself in predominantly male settings)

27. Mentorship Experience: _____

(Experience as a mentor or mentee in cybersecurity)

28. Diversity Advocacy: _____

(Involvement in promoting diversity and inclusion in tech)

29. Resilience: _____

(Ability to overcome challenges and biases in the workplace)

30. Networking Skills: _____

(Comfort in building professional relationships in the industry)

How to Use the Assessment Form

- **Set Aside Uninterrupted Time:** Find a quiet space to reflect on your skills without distractions.

- **Be Honest with Yourself:** This assessment is for your benefit. Overestimating or underestimating your skills won't help you grow.

- **Consider Recent Experiences:** When rating your skills, consider recent projects or situations where you've applied these abilities.

- **Don't Compare Yourself to Others:** This is about your personal growth, not how you measure up to your colleagues.

- **Take Notes:** As you go through each skill, jot down specific examples or areas you'd like to improve. These notes will be valuable when creating your development plan.

Interpreting Your Results

After completing the assessment, Identify your top 5 strengths. These are your standout skills. Consider how you can leverage these in your current role or pursue new opportunities. Additionally, you should:

- **Identify 3 Areas for Improvement:** Your growth opportunities are the areas where you scored the lowest. Don't view them as weaknesses but as areas for exciting development.

- **Look for Patterns:** Are your technical skills stronger than your soft skills, or vice versa? This can help you understand where to focus your development efforts.

- **Consider Your Career Goals:** How do your current skills align with where you want to be in 1, 5, or 10 years?

Creating a Personal Development Plan

Now that you have a clear picture of your skills, it's time to create an action plan:

- **Set SMART Goals:** For each area you want to improve, set Specific, Measurable, Achievable, Relevant, and Time-bound goals.

- **Identify Resources:** Research courses, books, mentorship opportunities, or projects that can help you develop your target skills.

- **Create a Timeline:** Break down your goals into manageable steps with deadlines.

- **Find An Accountability Partner:** Share your goals with a mentor, colleague, or friend who can support and motivate you.

- **Plan for Obstacles:** Anticipate potential challenges and how you'll overcome them.

Strategies for Skill Enhancement

- **Continuous Learning:** Stay updated with the latest cybersecurity trends through online courses, webinars, and industry publications.
- **Hands-on Practice:** Set up a home lab to experiment with new technologies and techniques.
- **Networking:** Attend industry events and join professional organizations to learn from peers and stay informed about job opportunities.
- **Mentorship:** Seek out mentors who can guide your career development and provide valuable insights.
- **Volunteer:** Offer your skills to non-profit organizations or open-source projects to gain experience and make a positive impact.

Overcoming Challenges in Skill Development

Remember, as women and minorities in cybersecurity, we face unique challenges, including:

- **Imposter Syndrome:** Remember that feeling like an imposter often means pushing yourself to grow. Acknowledge your achievements and the value you bring.
- **Lack of Representation:** Seek role models and mentors who share your background. If you can't find them locally, look for virtual mentorship opportunities or online communities.

- **Bias and Stereotypes:** Focus on your skills and achievements. Document your successes and be prepared to advocate for yourself.

- **Work-Life Balance:** Set boundaries & prioritize self-care to avoid burnout.

- **Limited Access to Resources:** Search for scholarships, grants, or employer-sponsored training programs to support your skill development.

Reassessment and Continuous Growth

The cybersecurity landscape is constantly evolving, and so should your skills, so plan to reassess yourself regularly using these four steps:

1. Schedule quarterly progress check-ins and adjust your goals if needed.

2. Annually retake this full assessment to track your growth over time.

3. Stay flexible and willing to pivot as new technologies and threats emerge.

4. Celebrate your wins, no matter how small. Every step forward is a victory.

Cultural Influences & Self Awareness

Growing up in a culture that valued modesty and discouraged self-promotion, I often underestimated my abilities. It took me years to realize that this cultural conditioning was holding me back in my career. Many come from backgrounds that may influence how we view and limit ourselves. Below are some ways your culture may hinder you:

Collectivist Cultures: This culture emphasizes group harmony over individual achievement; you might find it uncomfortable to highlight your personal strengths.

Gender Repressive Cultures: In many cultures, women are socialized to be modest and self-effacing. This can lead to underestimating our abilities and achievements.

Authoritative Cultures: Some cultures place a high value on respecting authority, which might make it difficult for you to accurately assess your skills relative to those in higher positions.

Cultural Concepts of Success: Some cultures value certain jobs as a badge of honor or success. A career in tech or cybersecurity may not align with the skills valued in your community, leading to a mismatch in how you view and assess yourself.

Strategies for Overcoming Cultural Barriers in Self-Assessment

- **Seek Out Diverse Perspectives:** Don't rely solely on your own assessment. Gather feedback from colleagues, mentors, and peers from different cultural backgrounds to ensure you have an accurate 360-View of you.

- **Practice Positive Self-Talk:** Challenge cultural messages that encourage excessive modesty. Remind yourself that recognizing your strengths isn't boasting – it's an essential part of professional growth.

- **Use Objective Measures:** Use concrete achievements and metrics to assess your skills. This can help overcome cultural biases towards modesty.

- **Rethink Self-Promotion:** If self-promotion feels uncomfortable, try thinking of it as sharing information that could help others or contribute to team success because this is true.

- **Educate Others:** Help your colleagues and superiors understand how cultural differences might impact self-assessment and communication styles.

- **Embrace Your Unique Perspective:** Remember that your cultural background gives you a unique lens to approach cybersecurity challenges. This is a strength, not a weakness.

Case Studies: Skills Assessment in Action

Here are a couple of real-world examples of how skills assessment has made a difference for women in cybersecurity:

Case Study 1: Maria's Journey to Leadership

Maria, a Latina cybersecurity analyst, had always excelled in her technical role but struggled to see herself in leadership. After completing a comprehensive skills assessment, she was surprised to find that her communication, problem-solving, and team collaboration scores were exceptionally high. This revelation gave Maria the confidence to apply for a team leader position. She leveraged her newly recognized strengths in her application and interview, articulating how her unique perspectives as a woman of color would benefit the team. Maria not only got the position but excelled in it, bringing a fresh approach to team management that improved her overall performance.

Case Study 2: Aisha's Career Pivot

Aisha, a Black woman with a background in network security, felt stuck in her career. She loved cybersecurity but wasn't sure how to progress. After conducting a skills inventory, she realized she knew how to explain complex concepts in simple terms. She had developed this skill through years of translating tech jargon for her non-technical family members. Recognizing this strength, Aisha pivoted her career towards cybersecurity education and awareness. She started by creating internal training programs for her company, which were so successful that she was eventually promoted to lead the company's entire cybersecurity awareness initiative. Today, Aisha is a sought-after speaker and consultant, helping organizations build strong security cultures.

Case Study 3: Sarah

Sarah Thompson's journey as a dedicated cybersecurity professional highlights the power of self-assessment.

As a mid-level cybersecurity analyst, Sarah felt her career had plateaued. She realized that to stay relevant, she needed to re-evaluate her skills and identify areas for growth. Using personal self-assessment, Sarah looked closer at her technical skills, soft skills, and certifications. She discovered gaps in AI and machine learning and identified a need to improve her leadership and communication skills.

Sarah then created a development plan and began enrolling in AI and ML courses. She also pursued CISSP and CEH certifications and joined a Toastmasters club. Sarah began taking on new leadership opportunities within her company's women in tech ERG. Soon after taking these critical steps, Sarah was promoted to a senior analyst role, leading her team to integrate AI and ML into the company's security infrastructure. As a new lead analyst, she began mentoring other women in cybersecurity and became a staunch advocate for inclusive hiring practices.

Sarah's story demonstrates the impact of self-assessment and continuous learning. By taking stock of her skills and addressing gaps, she advanced her career and significantly impacted her organization and the cybersecurity community.

Each of these stories is a good reminder that self-assessment is always a starting point when you seek ways to grow and advance in your career. Use it to guide your learning and development, but don't let it limit your aspirations. The cybersecurity field is vast, and there's always room to grow and excel.

Your journey in cybersecurity is uniquely yours. Embrace it, shape it, and never stop growing. The digital world needs your voice, your skills, and your leadership. It's time to make your mark.

CHAPTER SIXTEEN

MASTERING THE
CYBERSECURITY INTERVIEW

"Success is where preparation and opportunity meet."

~Bobby Unser

Whether you're eyeing an entry-level, specialist, or analyst position, this chapter is your compass in the complex terrain of cybersecurity job hunting.

A Field of Opportunity and Challenge

Let's start with some good news. The cybersecurity job market is booming! With an estimated 3.5 million unfilled cybersecurity jobs globally, you might think landing a position would be a walk in the park. But while demand is high, so are the stakes. Companies are searching for skilled professionals who can hit the ground running, making entry-level positions rare and fiercely competitive.

Cybersecurity isn't just a job; it's a vital shield protecting critical systems and sensitive information from an ever-evolving array of digital threats. It encompasses infrastructure, network, cloud, and application security. At its core, cybersecurity is about safeguarding confidentiality, integrity, and availability of data and resources through authentication, authorization, auditing, and encryption controls. The demand for cybersecurity professionals is so high that the White House has highlighted cybersecurity jobs as a key part of the proposed American Jobs Plan. According to Cyber Seek, nearly half a million current cybersecurity positions are waiting to be filled across the United States.

Compensation Snapshot

Now, let's talk about compensation. As a mid-level position with room for advancement, cybersecurity analysts are well-compensated. According to Cyber Seek, the average salary for a cybersecurity analyst is $107,500. However, it's worth noting that Dice's latest Tech Salary Report puts the average at $96,379, showing a 5.7 percent decline between 2021 and 2022. But don't let this dip discourage you. It's likely a result of more people entering the field, which can temporarily ease demand. Trust me, the opportunities remain plentiful.

Preparing for An Interview

Interviewing for a cybersecurity position is a unique challenge. It not only requires showcasing your technical prowess; you must also demonstrate your problem-solving skills, communication abilities, and cultural fitness. As someone on both sides of the interview table, I can tell you that preparation is key.

Start by optimizing your LinkedIn profile, highlighting your cybersecurity experience, certifications, and endorsements. Another good way to get noticed is by actively participating in cybersecurity groups and discussions. It's also a great way to stay current on industry trends.

Dressing the Part:
It's More Than the Right Clothes

Dress the part before you even get the part. Let me share a personal anecdote. I had a virtual interview for a cybersecurity analyst position early in my career. Thinking I could get away with a professional top and pajama bottoms, I confidently logged into the video call. Midway through the interview, I had to stand up to adjust my camera, revealing my less-than-professional lower half. Needless to say, I didn't get that job. The lesson? Whether in-person or virtual, dress for success. It's not just about looking good; it's about feeling confident and presenting yourself as a professional. For in-person interviews, I always err on the side of caution. A pair of slacks, a crisp shirt, and polished shoes have never let me down. Of course, I dress professionally from head to toe for virtual interviews or talks now because you never know when you might need to stand up.

Speaking the Language

Communication is crucial in cybersecurity. You need to be able to explain complex concepts to both technical and non-technical audiences. I've found that practicing my explanations beforehand helps immensely. It helps to try explaining a cybersecurity concept to a friend or family member who is not in the field. If they can understand it, you're likely on the right track.

In one of my previous interviews, I recall being asked to explain the concept of a DDoS attack to a hypothetical CEO who had no technical background. Drawing on my practice sessions, I used an analogy of a busy restaurant overwhelmed by a flash mob of customers. My ability to simplify complex ideas impressed the interviewer, which set me apart from other candidates.

Showcasing Your Technical Chops

Of course, technical skills are the backbone of any cybersecurity role. Be prepared to discuss and demonstrate your knowledge of key concepts, tools, and methodologies. Here's a pro tip: Don't just recite definitions. Share real-world applications and experiences.

When asked about encryption, I once interviewed a candidate who didn't just define symmetric and asymmetric encryption. Instead, they shared a story about implementing PGP encryption for a previous employer's email system, detailing the challenges and solutions. That practical experience made all the difference.

Preparing for Technical Questions

While we've covered some interview questions earlier, let me share six specific technical questions that hiring managers often ask cybersecurity analyst candidates:

1. How do you define a threat or vulnerability on a network?

2. What is a DDoS attack? How can you minimize it quickly?

3. What is a CIA triad?

4. Explain the importance of DNS monitoring.

5. Can you explain SSL?

6. If you needed to encrypt and compress data for transmission, which would you do first and why?

As you ponder these questions, I want you to keep in mind what Wendy Liu, Partner, and Managing Director at IT Employment Solutions Provider at Vaco, once told me, "Successful interviewees are prepared to provide thorough real-life examples of recent projects where they have solved similar challenges to those faced by the company they are interviewing with." Don't just give textbook answers. Relate your responses to your personal experiences and contributions.

Understanding the Company's Technology Stack

Do your homework on the company's technology and platforms before the interview. David Galownia, CEO of IT services company Slingshot, advises, "Do research on the specifics of the company. This doesn't mean just figuring out their culture and values. If possible, figure out how they develop. What's their process: Agile or waterfall? What do their timelines look like for a project? What's the team structure?"

This level of knowledge will allow you to tailor your responses and show how you can seamlessly fit into their development process. Don't worry if you're not familiar with all their tools. A well-rounded understanding of cybersecurity principles can help you navigate these discussions.

What Companies Look for in a Cybersecurity Analyst

In my conversations with hiring managers, I've identified five key qualities they often seek in cybersecurity analyst candidates:

1. Experience at a company dealing with highly sensitive data

2. Strong project management skills

3. Strong experience with security tooling

4. Ability to script or write code

5. Experience at a highly regarded security firm

Remember, cybersecurity analysts often work as internal consultants. If you have consulting experience, highlight it; it's excellent preparation for this role.

Leveraging Online Resources and Communities

In my journey through the cybersecurity landscape, I've found that knowledge shared by peers can be invaluable. The internet is a treasure trove of resources for aspiring cybersecurity professionals. Here's some of my favorite online platforms that have helped me prepare for interviews and stay current in the field:

- **Reddit's r/cybersecurity and r/netsec communities** are goldmines of information. I've found discussions about recent interview experiences, tips on handling technical questions, and advice on navigating the job market. These forums have given me insights that no textbook could provide.

- Platforms like TryHackMe and HackTheBox have been instrumental in more structured learning and interview preparation. They offer hands-on challenges that simulate real-world scenarios, which is exactly the experience that impresses interviewers. I remember tackling a particularly tricky challenge on HackTheBox just days before an interview. When a similar scenario occurred during the technical assessment, I felt like I had an ace.

- Capture the Flag (CTF) activities offer numerous benefits for new cybersecurity or mid-level individuals, including hands-on experience with real-world cybersecurity challenges. Participants get to apply theoretical knowledge in a controlled, gamified environment, which helps solidify their understanding of various cybersecurity concepts.

Staying Current: The Cybersecurity Professional's Lifeline

In the ever-evolving world of cybersecurity, staying up to date isn't just a good practice; it's a necessity. I learned this lesson the hard way when, during an interview, I was asked about my thoughts on a major data breach that had occurred just the week before.

I had been so focused on preparing for technical questions that I neglected to keep up with current events. I didn't get that job. Since then, I've made it a habit to stay informed about the latest cybersecurity trends, major breaches, and emerging technologies. I start each day by scanning cybersecurity news sites like *The Hacker News, Krebs on Security*, and *Dark Reading*. This daily ritual has prepared me for interviews and made me more effective in my day-to-day work.

Podcasts have also become another valuable resource for me. Shows like "Risky Business" and "Security Now" are great for staying informed during my work commute or while doing chores. They often feature discussions on recent breaches and emerging threats, providing insights I can bring up in interviews to demonstrate my engagement with the field.

Attending cybersecurity conferences, even virtually, is incredibly valuable. These events offer a glimpse into cutting-edge research and emerging trends. Plus, they're great networking opportunities. I've been blessed to land more than one interview through connections made at conferences.

Mastering the Remote Interview

The landscape of job interviews has changed dramatically in recent years, with remote interviews increasingly becoming the norm. I can still remember my very first virtual interview. I was so focused on the technical aspects that I completely overlooked the unique challenges of a virtual format. First and foremost, don't forget to test your technology beforehand.

I once had my internet cut out while explaining how I would respond to a DDoS attack. The irony wasn't lost on me and certainly didn't impress the interviewer. Now, I always do a test run with the specific platform the company is using, whether it's Zoom, Microsoft Teams, or another tool.

Your environment matters more than you might think. I learned this when I had an impromptu interview while visiting my family. I called from a guest room with questionable lighting and a less-than-professional background. I always ensure a clean, well-lit space with a neutral background for video calls. If you're in a pinch, most video conferencing software offers virtual backgrounds; test them first to avoid glitchy surprises.

Body language is even more important during a virtual interview. Make a conscious effort to maintain eye contact by looking directly into the camera, not at the screen. Also, pay attention to your posture and use hand gestures naturally, just as you would in an in-person interview.

One advantage of remote interviews is that you can have notes or resources at hand without the interviewer seeing them. However, be careful not to rely on them too heavily. I once fumbled an answer because I was reading my notes instead of engaging in the conversation. Now, I keep only brief bullet points nearby as reminders, focusing on maintaining a natural dialogue.

Lastly, don't forget to follow up after the interview. In a remote setting, it's even more important to reaffirm your interest in the position and thank the interviewer for their time. It's best to send a brief email within 24 hours, highlighting key points from your discussion and expressing your continued enthusiasm for the role.

Remote interviews may feel different, but with the right preparation, you can make a strong impression and showcase your cybersecurity expertise, regardless of the format.

The Value of Certifications

While we've focused a lot on experience and skills, I'd be remiss if I didn't mention the importance of certifications yet again. Some valuable certifications for cybersecurity analysts include:

- Certified Information Systems Security Professional (CISSP)
- Certified Information Systems Auditor (CISA)
- Certified Information Privacy Professional (CIPP)
- SANS/GIAC Certification
- CompTIA Security+
- Certified Information Security Manager (CISM)
- GIAC Certified Incident Handler (GCIH)
- GIAC Security Essentials Certification

Many job postings explicitly request these certifications, and having them can certainly give you an edge. However, don't be discouraged if you're still working on them. The demand for cybersecurity professionals is so intense that some employers overlook the certification prerequisite if you can show the necessary skills and experience.

If you have certifications, be prepared to discuss how you've applied the skills they represent in real-world scenarios. If you're still working on them, show your commitment to continuous learning and outline your certification goals.

Embrace the Journey

As we wrap up this chapter, I want to emphasize that each interview is a learning experience. Even if you don't get the job, you gain valuable insights into the industry, your strengths, and areas for improvement.

Remember, cybersecurity is a field that rewards continuous learning and adaptability. Show your interviewers what you know and your capacity and enthusiasm for growth. Your next great opportunity is out there.

You must prepare and approach each interview with confidence, authenticity, and a genuine passion for protecting our digital world. The world is awaiting your contribution to the next BIG idea. You've got this!

CONCLUSION

A s we conclude our journey on a high note, we must still confront the elephant in the room. The Tech cybersecurity fields remain stubbornly homogeneous despite the industry's proclaimed commitment to Diversity, Equity, and Inclusion (DEI). The statistics tell a stark story. Women comprise only 24% of the cybersecurity workforce, Black professionals only 9%, and Hispanic professionals only 4%. This isn't just underrepresentation; it's a crisis of exclusion that weakens our national security and innovation potential.

We cannot create a better future by ignoring the obvious. Women and minorities face unique challenges, barriers, and biases in tech and cybersecurity fields. While the industry bemoans a cybersecurity talent gap with thousands of unfilled positions, it maintains structures and practices that exclude qualified, diverse candidates. This paradox exposes a fundamental flaw in how the industry approaches talent acquisition and development. The path forward will require more than just acknowledgment. It demands action, and each of us has a part to play:

Industry Leaders and Organizations

- Implement transparent pay equity policies and regular audits.
- Create specific leadership development programs for women of color.

- Establish mentorship and sponsorship programs that specifically support underrepresented groups.
- Set measurable diversity goals for hiring and promotion, with accountability measures.

Educational Institutions

- Expand K-12 cybersecurity education programs, especially in underserved communities.
- Create early exposure programs that show young girls and students of color that they belong in tech.
- Develop scholarship programs specifically for women and minorities in cybersecurity.
- Partner with industry to create clear pathways from education to employment.

Current Cybersecurity Professionals

- Actively mentor and sponsor women, especially women of color
- Challenge discriminatory practices and policies in your workplace.
- Share your experiences and success stories to inspire others.
- Create or join employee resource groups focused on diversity in cybersecurity.

Aspiring Cybersecurity Professionals

- Utilize this book's technical and strategic guidance to build your skills.
- Connect with professional organizations focused on women and minorities in tech.

- Document and share your journey to inspire others.

The future of tech and cybersecurity holds magnificent promise if we tap into all available talent, regardless of gender, race, or background. Our diverse perspectives will help combat increasingly sophisticated cyber threats. Therefore, we cannot afford to exclude brilliant minds based on outdated biases and systemic barriers.

To my sisters in tech, especially women of color, your presence in this field is transforming an industry that desperately needs your perspectives and expertise. Your challenges are real, but so is your power to drive change. Remember, this book isn't just a guide. It's a call for revolution. Every time you succeed, persist, and lift another sister up, you're building the foundation for the next generation of diverse women leaders.

To industry Allies and Thought Leaders, leverage your platforms to help reshape the face of the industry literally and figuratively. The current 3.5M unfilled cybersecurity positions worldwide represent more than just job openings. They represent 3.5M opportunities to shatter glass ceilings. We have the tools, we know the solutions, and now we must act.

Your Next Power Move

- Share this book with more women, especially women of color, who are interested in pursuing a career in tech or cybersecurity.

- Join or create local initiatives to introduce young girls to technology and cybersecurity.

- Document and celebrate the achievements of women in cybersecurity.

- Mentor at least one woman of color who is interested in entering the field.

Rise Up and Act! The Tech and Cybersecurity industry cannot reach its highest peak until the field is as diverse as the society it protects.

Take the Breaking the Code Pledge

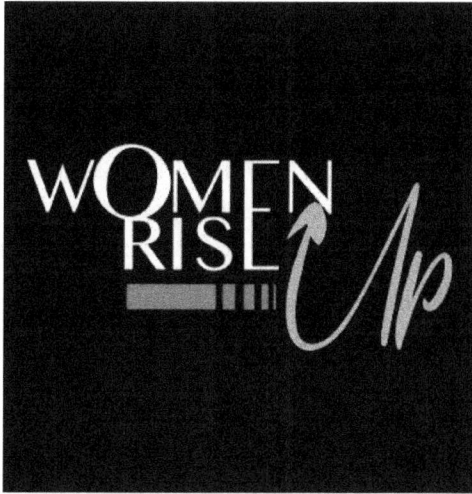

I pledge to take an active role in transforming the cybersecurity and tech industry by committing to the following actions:

1. **Championing Diversity and Inclusion:** I will actively promote and advocate for equal opportunities and representation for underrepresented groups in cybersecurity and technology, particularly women and women of color.

2. **Mentoring and Sponsoring Future Leaders**: I will dedicate time and effort to mentor and sponsor women, especially women of color, to empower them to advance and excel in their careers. I will share my knowledge, experience, and network to support their growth.

3. **Standing Against Discrimination**: I will courageously speak out against and challenge discriminatory practices

and policies in the workplace and industry. I will create a culture of respect, equity, and inclusion.

4. **Continuous Learning and Knowledge Sharing:** I will commit to staying informed about the latest trends and developments in cybersecurity. I will actively share my knowledge and experiences to inspire and uplift others, fostering a culture of continuous learning and innovation.

5. **Creating Inclusive and Supportive Environments:** I will strive to build inclusive, safe, and supportive environments where all individuals, regardless of their background, feel seen, heard, and valued. I will encourage collaboration and celebrate diverse perspectives.

6. **Advocating for Systemic Change:** I will advocate for policies and initiatives promoting diversity, inclusion, and equity within cybersecurity and technology. I will work towards dismantling barriers and systemic biases that hinder the advancement of women and underrepresented groups.

7. **Claiming My Space and Owning My Power:** I will boldly claim my space in the cybersecurity industry and own my power as a catalyst for change. I will encourage others to do the same, fostering a community of empowered and confident individuals.

Breaking the Code is about the people who make a difference and impact change. The key to breaking the code is YOU.

Together, we can build a diverse, innovative, and inclusive cybersecurity industry that empowers the next generation of women in technology.

Signature: _____

Date: _____

ABOUT THE AUTHOR

Dr. **Cheryl Cooper** is a trailblazing United States Navy Veteran, renowned for her transformative leadership in cybersecurity. She is a distinguished and motivational global speaker, podcaster, coach, author, educator and scholar with nearly three decades of experience in cybersecurity and telecommunications. Driven by her passion for mentorship, Dr. Cooper founded the non-profit organization Women in CyberSecurity (WiCyS) of the greater Kansas City Metroplex. Through her tireless efforts, she has championed countless underserved high school students, providing them with visibility and opportunities in the tech industry. As the host of the podcast "Ctrl+Alt+Em-Power," Dr. Cooper unlocks the critical intersections of cyber resilience, technology, and inclusion. She has delivered numerous keynotes on topics such as cyber resilience, managing cybersecurity threats, security awareness, security and privacy implications on worldwide pandemics, as well as keynoting on the keys to unlock the code to build the next generation of women in cybersecurity and technology.

Dr. Cooper is highly sought after for her expertise in mentoring and building inclusive technology communities. As a national thought leader on closing the gap for women and underrepresented groups in STEM, Dr. Cooper has been tapped to share her perspectives on several notable panels, including the Women in Telecom Conference, held following the September 11th attacks.

Dr. Cooper is a Business Information Security Officer at a Fortune 100 company and a computer science adjunct professor. She holds a Doctorate in Computer Sciences and is a Certified Information Systems Security Professional (CISSP). Her dissertation, which focused on the growing problem of information privacy management and its variation by age group, has significant implications for current debates about security and privacy with smartphones and IoT devices. Dr. Cooper also serves as President of Women in CyberSecurity (WiCyS) Kansas City Metroplex, an organization dedicated to encouraging young girls and women to pursue careers in STEM.

In 2019, Dr. Cooper was awarded the Central Exchange Woman in Science, Technology, Engineering, & Mathematics (STEM) Women's Champion award. She was also recognized for a second time by the Central Exchange STEM Champion for her visionary "Groundbreaking" leadership in gender equality in STEM in 2024.

Her many accolades are a testament to her passion for service and unwavering dedication to mentoring those who are marginalized and underrepresented.

In her powerful memoir, **Hood to Hooded: A Black Woman's Choice to Rise**, Dr. Cooper explores unjust racial and gender biases in corporate America. Her moving personal journey is an inspiring story of advocacy that has resonated with many and provides hope for generations to come.

Connect with Dr. Cheryl Cooper
@https://www.drcherylcooper.com.

Your Reflections, Notes, and Personal Action Plan

Your Reflections, Notes, and Personal Action Plan

_____

_____

_____

_____

_____

_____

_____

_____

_____

_____

_____

_____

_____

_____

_____

_____

_____

_____

_____

_____

_____

_____

_____

_____

_____

_____

_____

_____

YOUR REFLECTIONS, NOTES, AND PERSONAL ACTION PLAN

_____

_____

_____

_____

_____

_____

_____

_____

_____

_____

_____

_____

_____

_____

_____

_____

_____

_____

_____

_____

_____

_____

_____

_____

YOUR REFLECTIONS, NOTES, AND PERSONAL ACTION PLAN

_____
_____
_____
_____
_____
_____
_____
_____
_____
_____
_____
_____
_____
_____
_____
_____
_____
_____
_____
_____
_____
_____
_____

YOUR REFLECTIONS, NOTES, AND PERSONAL ACTION PLAN

_____

_____

_____

_____

_____

_____

_____

_____

_____

_____

_____

_____

_____

_____

_____

_____

_____

_____

_____

_____

_____

_____

_____

_____

Your Reflections, Notes, and Personal Action Plan

BONUS MATERIAL

Discover More with Ctrl+Alt+Em-POWER Podcast - Empowering Women in Cybersecurity and Technology

Join me, Dr. Cheryl Cooper, as I share personal stories, expert insights, and interviews with trailblazing women who are redefining what's possible in cyber and tech.
Together, we'll explore topics like:
Building confidence and resilience in male-dominated spaces.
Navigating career transitions and breaking into cybersecurity.
Strategies for growth, leadership, and personal empowerment.

How to Listen
Scan the QR code below to access my podcast directly from your device. Whether you're commuting, taking a break, or seeking a motivational boost, Ctrl+Alt+Em-POWER is here to keep you inspired.

Let's Em-POWER Your Journey!

Want to connect further? Visit drcherylcooper.com for more resources, book updates, and exclusive content.

Dr. Cheryl COOPER

Dr. Cheryl Cooper, CISSP,
President WiCyS Kansas City
Website: www.drcherylcooper.com

Ctrl + Alt
+ Em-Power
with Dr. Cheryl Cooper

SCAN TO TUNE IN NOW!

BIBLIOGRAPHY

American Psychological Association. "*How Bystanders Can Shut Down Microaggressions*." APA Monitor on Psychology, September 2021. https://www.apa.org/monitor/2021/09/feature-bystanders-microaggressions Brown, Brené.

The Gifts of Imperfection: *"Let Go of Who You Think You're Supposed to Be and Embrace Who You Are."* Center City: Hazelden Publishing, 2010.

Colorism Project. "*Journal of Colorism Studies.*" Accessed January 6, 2025. https://colorismproject.com/journal-of-colorism.

Covey, Stephen R. The *"7 Habits of Highly Effective People: Powerful Lessons in Personal Change."* New York: Free Press, 2004.

Cuncic, Arlin. "*What Is Imposter Syndrome?*" Verywell Mind, January 19, 2024.https://www.verywellmind.com/imposter-syndrome-and-social-anxiety-disorder-4156469.

Cybersecurity & Infrastructure Security Agency. *"The Role of the Security Analyst."* 2024. http://www.cisa.gov.

DeVille, K. *"STEM Education Statistics in 2024."* STEM Education Guide, January 16, 2024. https://stemeducationguide.com/stem-education-statistics/.

Drucker, Peter F. *"Management Challenges for the 21st Century."* New York: HarperBusiness, 1999.

Enterprise Apps Today. *"AI in Cybersecurity: Current Applications and Future Trends."* 2024. https://www.enterpriseappstoday.com/stats/ai-in-cybersecurity-statistics.html.

Frost, R. 6 *"Cybersecurity Skills You Need to Know."* Coursera (blog), July 20, 2021. https://www.coursera.org/articles/cybersecurity-skills.

Fruhlinger, Josh. *"How to Become a CISO: Leadership Tips from Top Security Executives."* CSO Online, April 3, 2023. https://www.csoonline.com/article/3391990/how-to-become-a-ciso-leadership-tips-from-top-security-executives.html.

Fruhlinger, Josh, and Charles Brumfield. *"The 15 Biggest Data Breaches of the 21st Century."* CSO Online, January 26, 2023. https://www.csoonline.com/article/2130877/the-biggest-data-breaches-of-the-21st-century.html.

Gartner. *"Gartner Predicts 60% of Organizations Will Use Cybersecurity Risk as a Primary Determinant in Conducting Third-Party Transactions and Business Engagements by 2025."* June 7, 2023. https://www.gartner.com/en/newsroom/press-releases/2023-06-07-gartner-predicts-60-percent-of-organizations-will-use-cybersecurity-risk-as-primary-determinant.

Gates, Melinda. *"The Moment of Lift: How Empowering Women Changes the World."* New York: Flatiron Books, 2019.

Guynn, Jessica. *"We Need to Talk About the Macro Effect of Microaggressions on Women at Work."* USA TODAY, September 7, 2024. https://www.usatoday.com/story/money/2023/10/05/microaggressions-women-at-work-new-study/71005816007/.

Harvard Business Review. *"When and How to Respond to Microaggressions."* July 2020. https://hbr.org/2020/07/when-and-how-to-respond-to-microaggressions.

Imes, Suzanne, and Pauline R. Clance. *"The Impostor Phenomenon in High Achieving Women: Dynamics and Therapeutic Intervention."* Psychotherapy Theory, Research and Practice 15, no. 3 (1978): 241-247.

InfoSec Institute. *"Understanding the Role of Security Engineers."* 2024. http://www.infosecinstitute.com.

ISACA. *"Governance, Risk, and Compliance (GRC) Explained."* 2024. http://www.isaca.org.

Katsikas, Sokratis K., Fábio Silva, Vassilis Fotopoulos, and Georgios Vardoulias. *"Automating Incident Response in IoT Environments Using Machine Learning."* Future Internet 13, no. 3 (2021): 57.

Kulacaoglu, F., and S. Kose. *"Borderline Personality Disorder (BPD): In the Midst of Vulnerability, Chaos, and Awe."* Brain Sciences 8, no. 11 (2018): 201.

Levy, Steven. New York: Anchor Press/Doubleda *"Hackers: Heroes of the Computer Revolution."* y, 1984.

Miessler, Daniel. *"The Real Reason to Learn to Code."* Daniel Miessler (blog), May 15, 2020. https://danielmiessler.com/blog/the-real-reason-to-learn-to-code/.

Mitnick, Kevin, and William L. Simon. *"Ghost in the Wires: My Adventures as the World's Most Wanted Hacker."* New York: Little, Brown and Company, 2011.

National Cybersecurity Institute. *"Cybersecurity Career Paths: A Guide for Professionals."* 2024. http://www.nationalcybersecurityinstitute.org.

Offensive Security. *"What Is Penetration Testing?"* 2024. http://www.offensive-security.com.

Patsakis, Constantinos, and Francisco Casino. *"Hydras and IPFS: A Decentralized Playground for Malware."* International Journal of Information Security 18, no. 6 (2019): 787-799.

Pew Research Center. *"What Makes a Good Leader, and Does Gender Matter?"* January 14, 2015. https://www.pewresearch.org/social-trends/2015/01/14/chapter-2-what-makes-a-good-leader-and-does-gender-matter/.

Psychology Today. *"The Detrimental Effects of Microaggressions."* October 2021. https://www.psychologytoday.com/us/blog/evidence-based-living/202110/the-detrimental-effects-microaggressions.

Sandberg, Sheryl. *"Lean In: Women, Work, and the Will to Lead."* New York: Alfred A. Knopf, 2013.

SANS Institute. *"Incident Response: Best Practices."* 2024. http://www.sans.org.

Schneier, Bruce. *"Kill Everybody: Security and Survival in a Hyper-Connected World."* New York: W. W. Norton & Company, 2018.

Smith, J. A., and R. L. Johnson. *"Colorism and Immigrant Earnings in the United States: A Quantitative Analysis."* Frontiers in Sociology 7 (2022): 1494236.

Sue, Derald Wing. *"Microaggressions in Everyday Life: Race, Gender, and Sexual Orientation."* Hoboken: John Wiley & Sons, 2010.

U.S. Bureau of Labor Statistics. *"Information Security Analysts."* In the Occupational Outlook Handbook. September 8, 2023. https://www.bls.gov/ooh/computer-and-information-technology/information-security-analysts.htm.

University of Washington. *"Addressing Microaggressions in the Classroom."* Teaching@UW. Accessed January 14, 2025. https://teaching.washington.edu/inclusive-teaching/addressing-microaggressions-in-the-classroom/.

World Economic Forum. *"Racial Equality and Skin Tone Bias: The Ongoing Issue of Colorism."* August 2020. https://www.weforum.org/stories/2020/08/racial-equality-skin-tone-bias-colourism/.

Yang, X.-M., H.-L. Liu, Z.-L. Liu, and X.-F. Zhao. *"A Novel Approach for Detecting Malware Based on Machine Learning."* *IEEE Access* 7 (2019): 9493-9502.

APPENDIX A

THE CODEBREAKERS GLOSSARY

T his comprehensive glossary covers both technical cybersecurity concepts and terms related to diversity and inclusion, providing readers with a well-rounded understanding of the key terms used throughout your book.

Note: This glossary is not an exhaustive list of all cybersecurity and diversity-related terms. Instead, it includes key terms relevant to the scope of this book, *Breaking the Code: Winning Strategies for Women in Cybersecurity & Tech*.

Access Control: The selective restriction of access to resources, ensuring only authorized individuals can access specific data or systems.

Advanced Persistent Threat (APT): A prolonged and targeted cyberattack in which an intruder gains access to a network and remains undetected for an extended period.

Artificial Intelligence (AI): The simulation of human intelligence processes by machines, used in cybersecurity for threat detection and response.

Authentication: The process of verifying the identity of a user, device, or system in a computer network.

Biometrics: The measurement and analysis of unique physical or behavioral characteristics for authentication purposes.

Blockchain: A decentralized, distributed ledger technology that records transactions across many computers to ensure data integrity and security.

Botnet: A network of private computers infected with malicious software and controlled as a group without the owners' knowledge.

Bug Bounty Program: An initiative that rewards individuals for finding and reporting software bugs and security vulnerabilities.

Cloud Security: The protection of data, applications, and infrastructure associated with cloud computing services.

Colorism: Prejudice or discrimination against individuals with darker skin tones, typically among people of the same ethnic or racial group.

Cryptography: The practice and study of techniques for secure communication and data protection in the presence of adversaries.

Cybersecurity: The practice of protecting systems, networks, and programs from digital attacks, involving technologies, processes, and practices designed to defend against, detect, and respond to threats.

Cyber Threat Intelligence: Information about potential or current attacks that threaten an organization, used to prepare, prevent, and identify cyber threats.

Data Breach: A security incident where sensitive, protected, or confidential data is accessed or used by an unauthorized individual.

Data Encryption Standard (DES): A symmetric-key algorithm for the encryption of digital data.

Denial of Service (DoS) Attack: An attack meant to shut down a machine or network, making it inaccessible to its intended users.

DevSecOps: A practice that integrates security into the DevOps software development process.

Diversity: The practice or quality of including people from a range of different social and ethnic backgrounds, genders, and sexual orientations.

Distributed Denial of Service (DDoS) Attack: An attack in which multiple compromised systems are used to target a single system, causing a denial of service.

Edge Computing: A distributed computing paradigm that brings computation and data storage closer to the sources of data.

Encryption: The process of encoding information so that only authorized parties can access it.

Endpoint Security: The practice of securing end-user devices such as desktops, laptops, and mobile devices from security threats.

Ethical Hacking: The practice of testing a computer system, network, or web application to find security vulnerabilities that a malicious hacker could potentially exploit.

Firewall: A network security system that monitors and controls incoming and outgoing network traffic based on predetermined security rules.

Identity and Access Management (IAM): A framework of policies and technologies for ensuring that the right individuals have the appropriate access to technology resources.

Imposter Syndrome: A psychological pattern in which an individual doubts their skills, talents, or accomplishments and fears being exposed as a "fraud".

Incident Response: An organized approach to addressing and managing the aftermath of a security breach or cyberattack.

Internet of Things (IoT): The interconnection via the internet of computing devices embedded in everyday objects, enabling them to send and receive data.

Intrusion Detection System (IDS): A device or software application that monitors a network or systems for malicious activity or policy violations.

Intrusion Prevention System (IPS): A network security/threat prevention technology that examines network traffic flows to detect and prevent vulnerability exploits.

Malware: Software designed to disrupt, damage, or gain unauthorized access to a computer system, including viruses, worms, trojans, and ransomware.

Mentorship: A relationship in which a more experienced person helps guide a less experienced person in their professional development.

Microaggression: Brief and commonplace verbal, behavioral, or environmental indignities that communicate hostile, derogatory, or negative attitudes toward marginalized groups.

Multi-Factor Authentication (MFA): A security system that requires more than one method of authentication to verify the user's identity.

Penetration Testing: An authorized simulated cyberattack on a computer system, performed to evaluate the security of the system.

Phishing: A cybercrime in which targets are contacted by someone posing as a legitimate institution to lure individuals into providing sensitive data.

Public Key Infrastructure (PKI): A set of roles, policies, and procedures needed to create, manage, distribute, use, store, and revoke digital certificates and manage public-key encryption.

Quantum Computing: A type of computing that uses quantum-mechanical phenomena to perform operations on data, potentially capable of breaking current encryption methods.

Ransomware: A type of malware that threatens to publish the victim's data or perpetually block access to it unless a ransom is paid.

Risk Assessment: The process of identifying, analyzing, and evaluating risk factors that could negatively impact an organization's information assets.

Sandbox: A testing environment that isolates untested code changes and experimentation from the production environment.

Security Awareness Training: Training provided to employees to help them understand the importance of cybersecurity and how to recognize and respond to potential threats.

Security Information and Event Management (SIEM): A system that combines security information management and security event management to provide real-time analysis of security alerts.

Security Operations Center (SOC): A centralized unit that deals with security issues on an organizational and technical level.

Social Engineering: The psychological manipulation of people into performing actions or divulging confidential information.

Social Engineering Attack: An attack that relies on human interaction and often involves tricking people into breaking normal security procedures.

STEM: An acronym for Science, Technology, Engineering, and Mathematics.

Threat Actor: An individual or entity responsible for an event or incident that impacts, or has the potential to impact, the safety or security of another entity.

Threat Hunting: The practice of proactively searching for cyber threats that are lurking undetected in a network.

Two-Factor Authentication (2FA): A security process in which the user provides two different authentication factors to verify themselves.

Unconscious Bias: Social stereotypes about certain groups of people that individuals form outside their own conscious awareness.

Virtual Private Network (VPN): A service that allows you to create a secure, encrypted connection to another network over the Internet.

Virtualization: The creation of a virtual version of something, such as a server, a storage device, or network resources.

Vulnerability: A weakness in a system that can be exploited by a threat actor to perform unauthorized actions within a computer system.

Whaling: A specific type of phishing attack that targets high-profile individuals, such as executives or senior management, within an organization.

Zero-Day Exploit: An attack that exploits a previously unknown vulnerability in a computer application or system.

Zero Trust Architecture: A security model that assumes no user, system, or service operating from within the security perimeter should be automatically trusted, requiring verification from everyone trying to access resources in the network.

www.ingramcontent.com/pod-product-compliance
Lightning Source LLC
Chambersburg PA
CBHW070352200326
41518CB00012B/2215